For the creativity, fun, caring, sharing, and support—
that comes from all good partnerships like ours.

PARTNERS FOR LEARNING

Promoting parent involvement in school

by
Janet Horowitz
and
Kathy Faggella

Art by
Kathy Faggella

FIRST TEACHER PRESS
First Teacher, Inc./Bridgeport, CT

ISBN 0-9615005-3-0

Library of Congress Catalog Card Number 86-82297

Design by Alice Cooke, A to Z Design, NYC

Cover Design by Alice Cooke; Illustration by Debby Dixler

Edited by Lisa Lyons Durkin

Associate Editor: Francesca DeMaria

Editorial Assistant: Kathleen Hyson

Technical Assistant: Michael Durkin

Manufactured in the United States of America.

Published by First Teacher Press, First Teacher, Inc.
P.O. Box 29, 60 Main Street, Bridgeport, CT 06602.

Distributed by: Gryphon House, Inc.
                  P.O. Box 275
                  Mt. Ranier, MD 20712

TABLE OF CONTENTS

TABLE OF CONTENTS

TAKING SCHOOL HOME

WE BELIEVE THAT

- education is a lifelong process.
- children are educated by the adults with whom they come in contact.
- parents want to be involved in their child's educational experience, but often they need to be shown how.
- parents and teachers are partners in a child's education.
- communication between the home and school is essential for the child's development.
- when parents participate in their child's school experience, everyone—the child, parents, and teachers—benefits.

OUR PHILOSOPHY

Education is a lifelong process. However, eighty percent of a person's lifetime learning takes place in the first six years, so parents and early childhood teachers have an important responsibility. They must work together to make sure that the children in their care develop into happy, healthy, independent individuals.

When they participate in their child's life at school,

PARENTS:

- Share experiences with their child without home interruptions
- Observe their child playing and working with other children and adults
- Begin to see their child in a new way with new abilities and skills
- Are better able to define appropriate levels of expectation for their child's development
- Have a basis to discuss "What did you do today in school?"
- Feel more comfortable with the learning environment they have chosen for their child
- Have the opportunity to informally discuss problems with the teacher
- Meet and compare notes with other parents with similar situations and concerns
- Get new ideas for games and projects to do at home
- Are reminded how much fun it is to play with their child
- Shine in the eyes of their child as they share special talents, skills, and hobbies with the whole class
- Develop parenting skills through workshops and parent/teacher conferences
- Feel good about themselves and their abilities as parents

When they involve parents in their program at school,

TEACHERS:

- Gain extra sets of helping hands
- Bring in more adult role models
- Enrich their curriculum with fresh new resources for teaching about careers, music, sports, different cultures, and so on
- Observe parent/child relationships and gain new understanding about children's behavior at school
- Cultivate a strong relationship with their "partners for learning"

"Parents and teachers work together to help children develop."

"Teachers gain valuable resources when they involve parents in the school program."

"Children feel special when their parents take the time to participate in their school experience."

When parents participate in their school experience, **CHILDREN**:

- Recognize the link between learning at school and at home
- See their parents as an intergral part of their learning experience
- Get to share their friends with their parents and vice versa
- See their parents in different roles
- Teach their parents about their daily school activities
- Share special, school-oriented experiences with their parents
- Show off their classroom and newly acquired skills
- Begin to feel the value of education when their parents take the time to visit and participate
- Feel special and cared about

HOW TO USE THIS BOOK

"Teachers must forge the vital link between home and school."

Partners for Learning assumes that children gain more from their school experience when their parents participate in that experience—and that parents really want to be involved in their children's education. This book is about how teachers can forge that vital link between home and school. It is organized into chapters which will help you to initiate, develop, and maintain a good working relationship with the parents of the children you teach.

The partnership between parents and teachers must be built on a firm foundation of trust. First and foremost, parents must develop confidence in the school they have selected for their child. Then, they need to feel welcome in the school and have the sense that you, the teacher, value their participation. They need to believe that they are still important in their child's education, even when that child is in school. They also must recognize you as a valuable resource for their child-rearing concerns. In time, they will realize why the link between home and school is so important to maintain.

"Tailor the activities and information in this book to meet your specific needs."

Use *Partners for Learning* as a guide and also as a resource for creative parent/child events and activities. Each school or center has its own special set of circumstances and thus the type of parent participation varies from place to place. Use the letters and invitations in this book as they are or tailor them to meet your specific needs. We have dealt with the issue of whether to refer to the child as he or she by alternating the use by chapter. However, you may wish to use he/she or s/he in your letters to go home if you and your parents feel more comfortable with this usage.

Create a Parent Communication Center in a small corner of the room or give parents a room of their own—let your space and parent group be your guide. Have special parent/child events at school monthly, bimonthly, or a few times annually. If all the parents in your school work during the day, reach out to grandparents and community members to be volunteers and schedule special events for early evening.

Above all, use this book to create an atmosphere in your school that makes parents feel as welcome and cared for as their children—an atmosphere that makes them feel like your partners for learning.

STARTING OUT RIGHT

HOME VISITS

A home visit by you, the teacher, helps bridge that initial gap between home and school. It gives you a chance to observe a child's home environment and perhaps to pick up some clues to the child's behavior in class. During the home visit, you can accomplish some of the following:

■ You can give parents some general information about the school's program and suggestions of things that they can do to prepare their child for the beginning of school (See page 16 for a sheet of suggestions that can be duplicated.)

■ You can give the child a colorful name tag to wear to school on the first day

■ You can take the child's picture for the class poster entitled "Our New Class." Children love to try to find their picture when they come into school. Immediately, they feel like they belong to the group.

■ You can help the child decide which of his favorite stuffed animals, dolls, or other prized possessions he should bring with him on the first day of school. By having a postive link to his home with him, he will often feel more secure at school.

Some parents may be reluctant to have a home visit. They might be anxious about how their house looks or feel like they are being "judged" by the teacher. To help alleviate these fears, you will want to send out a letter and/or call each of the families in your class in late August. A sample letter appears on the following page.

Dear Parents:

Before we know it, school will be starting and your child will be joining our class. I know that it's going to be a wonderful year and I'd like to start it out right by helping your child make the transition from your home to our class as easily as possible. One of the best ways that I've found for doing this is for me to visit your child at your home.

This visit will give your child a chance to meet me in a familiar, comfortable setting. He can show me some of the things that are important to him at home. He can introduce me to his brothers and sisters and pets so that I will know whom he is talking about when they are mentioned at school. If your child has any questions about coming to school, I'd like to answer them during this visit. Of course, I look forward to answering your questions, also.

Please consider which of the following visiting times would be most convenient for you and your child. I will call you soon to set up our meeting. I'm really looking forward to our visit. Thank you.

Sincerely,

Your child's teacher

Times _____

TIPS FOR PARENTS

As the beginning of the new school year approaches, parents are naturally concerned about having their child's first day of school work out well. Here are some suggestions for parents that will ease that initial transition from home to the classroom. You can send these tips home, give them to parents during a home visit, or you can distribute them during an orientation meeting.

MAKING THE FIRST DAY OF SCHOOL MORE COMFORTABLE

■ Be very positive about school in your talks with your child. Point out that you are excited about his going to school because it will be so much fun. Talk about school as a place where he will learn lots of new things. Talk about all the new playmates he will meet.

"Parents should be aware of their own fears about their child's new experience."

■ Become aware of your own concerns and fears about your child's new experience and his ability to handle it. If you are experiencing any fears, your child will tend to pick up on them and become scared as well. The best way to deal with your concerns is to remind yourself that your child will be fine—that you picked this school because you know that the staff will take good care of your child and that you will always be welcome to come into the school to talk to and work with the teacher if there are any problems.

"Parents can read books with their child about the first day of school."

■ Read some books together about the first day of school. Sharing a book gets your child to talk about his feelings and helps prepare him for this new experience. Try one of the following. These books should be available at your local library. If not, ask the librarian to suggest some others on this subject.
• *A Child Goes to School: A Storybook for Parents and Children Together* by Sara Bonnett Stein (Walker)
• *The First Day of School* by Marjorie Thayer (Children's Book Press)
• *The Berenstain Bears Go to School* by S. and J. Berenstain (Random House)
• *First Day in School* by Bill Binzen (Doubleday)
• *We Laughed a Lot the First Day of School* by Sylvia Tester (Child's World Inc.)
• *Sometimes I Don't Like School* by Paula Z. Hogan (Raintree Publishers)
• *Will I Have a Friend?* by Miriam Cohen (Macmillan)

■ Listen to your child's concerns, answer his questions, and reassure him that everything will be fine. If he expresses fears, do not deny them. Rather, be understanding about them and tell him that most people get scared before they try something new. Tell him about your own feelings when starting something new.

"Parents and children should visit school before it starts."

■ Visit the classroom together before school starts. Call the school to make sure someone will be there. Familiarize yourselves with the outside of the building as well as the inside.

■ On the first day of school, be sure to tell your child when you are leaving and when you will be back to pick him up.

■ If your child will be traveling by school bus or car pool, arrange for a practice run. Big yellow school buses can be frightening to young children so meet the bus driver and arrange to take a ride on the bus together. Read *Big Paul's School Bus* by Paul Nichols. If it is a car pool situation, be sure that your child knows who the driver is each day.

ORIENTATION MEETING

Parents need to trust and have confidence in you and in the entire school staff before they can freely leave their children in your care. That trust and confidence comes from getting to know you better and observing how you work with children. Therefore, there should be many opportunities for parents to get together with you, with and without their children.

One such opportunity is an orientation meeting for parents. Children should not be present at this time because their care might distract parents from really being able to participate. You might want to provide babysitting in another room.

"Use the orientation meeting to acquaint parents with your school and its policies."

During the orientation meeting, parents can become acquainted with the school/classroom and its policies. You might begin with an informal tour of the physical arrangement of the school. Use the tour to point out the children's cubbies and the various centers. In this way, you also will be letting parents know what your educational philosophy is. Then, get down to discussing the practical, day-to-day considerations that must be dealt with.

These things can include:
■ Your policy on the type of clothing children should wear (you must also tell parents what you do about outdoor play in cold and rainy weather)
■ Your policy on foods you offer and allow for snacks each day
■ Your policy on children's birthdays (See our suggestions on pages 61 and 62.)
■ Your policy on initial separation problems (do you allow parents to sit in the first few days, or do you scoot them out and promise to call them in 15 minutes, and so on)
■ Your policy on children who become ill during the school day (do you call parents to pick up the child or isolate them until pick-up time, or have a nurse on call)
■ Your policy on making up sick or absent days, if you have one
■ Your policy on pick-ups (procedures, where and with whom do the children go)

"Obtain important information for your records at the meeting."

Use the orientation meeting to obtain useful information for your records. Pass out 3" x 5" cards and pencils. Ask parents to fill in the following information:
■ Their names and phone numbers at home and work
■ The names and phone numbers of relatives and/or friends

who might be called in case of emergency when parents are not available
■ The names and phone numbers of the child's pediatrician and dentist
■ Any allergies the child might have
■ Any other information that might be needed to help the child learn, have fun, and be safe in your care

If you have one, point out your Parent Communication Center bulletin board, the scrap collecting box, and the parents' lending library. You might use this opportunity to tell parents about all the various ways they can help the school with volunteering and fundraising. Place sign-up sheets where parents can see them and encourage them to sign up, assuring them that they can easily get out of their obligation if they need to in the future.

The orientation meeting should allow parents to ask you any questions about the school and staff that might help them or their children adjust better.

Serve refreshments informally so that parents can talk with each other, you, and other members of the school staff. Let them move around the school or classroom and make their own observations. Be confident and friendly, accepting each parent for who he is. You will be dealing with them for a whole year and need to keep communication lines open.

Close the orientation meeting on a positive note by telling parents that they are always welcome to come to school to visit or volunteer.

After the orientation meeting and once school has begun, it's a nice idea to send a letter home to encourage parents to feel free to talk with you during the year. It is one more way to show parents that you want their participation and to encourage them to become involved in their child's education. There is a sample on the following page.

"Tell parents they are always welcome to visit or volunteer."

Dear Parents:

School has begun. Welcome.

I will be spending several hours each day with your child. I think we can help each other make it a wonderful year. You can help me work with your child at school; and perhaps I can offer you some tips on early childhood development and learning to use at home.

PLEASE STOP IN AND SAY HELLO to me at least once a week when you pick up or drop off your child. You also can check our bulletin board to find out what our week's themes and activities are (so that, when your child comes home from school, you know what you can ask about). While these drop-off/pick-up times are too hectic to get into important concerns — we can make an appointment for that — we can still chat a bit. I feel that the more we can touch base, the more comfortable we both will be to discuss your child's progress.

SEND ME NOTES. I'd like to hear about your child's comments about school, the positive as well as the negative. It feels good to hear about the things that your child likes — and productive to know about his dislikes. Let me know any changes in your child's behavior or attitude toward school. I like to keep an eye on the development of all of the children and any ideas or activities your child brings home from school. I'll try to get informative notes home to you, too, when I notice something new or if your child has had a special experience you should hear about.

I'm looking forward to working with you and having a great year with your child.

Sincerely yours,

Your child's teacher

STAYING IN TOUCH

COMMUNICATE!

PARENT COMMUNICATION CENTER

"Set up a center where parents can find important notices."

For a young child, making the break from home and parents, even for a few hours each day, can be a big step. It can also be traumatic for Mom and Dad! You can help open and maintain communications between the home and school by setting up a Parent Communication Center. This center is a place in the classroom where important information is posted just for parents. It should be situated near the pick-up and drop-off door and should be large enough to attract attention. Use this Parent Communication Center for posting notices about class activities—trips, special events, recipes, and other pertinent information. A large bulletin board, divided into different areas of interest, works well. It needs to be kept current enough to demand constant reviewing by parents.

A Parent Communication Center can include the following headings:

"Divide the communication center into different areas."

- READ THIS (child-rearing article)
- THEME OF THE WEEK/ACTIVITIES YOU CAN DO AT HOME— Please take one
- SCHOOL MAP/CLASS MAP
- PLEASE SAVE/SCRAP ITEM BOX
- TAKE-HOME EXPERIENCE CHART
- OUR NEWSLETTER—Please take one
- HAVE YOU SEEN THESE?
- BOOK CHECK OUT
- OUR TRIP
- YOU ARE INVITED
- WE NEED YOUR HELP
- PARENT-TO-PARENT

Read This!

Post articles relating to child-rearing and child development that might be useful to the parents. If you feel that many of the parents are concerned about or are having particular difficulties with one topic, you might want to copy an article and send it home with the children in addition to posting it.

**Theme of the Week/
Activities You Can
Do at Home—
Please take one**

Let parents know what you will be working on with the children during the week so that they can enrich and extend their children's learning at home. If possible, send home parent/child activity sheets that parents and children can work on together to extend and reinforce the learning taking place at school. You can make a "pocket" to put up on your bulletin board to store your "take-home" activity sheets. (See page 25 for directions.) These sheets also can cover activities that you as a teacher can't do at school (activities to be done at night, on weekends, in the kitchen, and so on).

School Map/Class Map

Make an illustrated map or layout of the school and class area, both inside and out. Children can show their parents where they "worked and played today." Make sure to include various equipment.

**Take-Home Experience
Chart**

Post a copy of this chart which enables parents to learn more about what their children have been doing in school. Through the process of making it, children can spend time recalling details and the sequence of events in the past week.

With the children, discuss the major activities of the week. Then, you write them out in sequential order. Include special trips, visitors, activities, crafts, and events. You can write out the chart on an 8½" X 11" sheet. It can be reproduced, written on mimeo stencils, or written with carbon paper so that each child gets a copy to take home that same day. Keep the master copy to post in your Communication Center. Children can draw their own pictures, designs, or colors that remind them of the week on their copy.

Vary the method of this experience chart. One week, you might save some representative objects from each day. Set them out on Friday to refresh memories. Then, write the chart. Another week, you might have each child contribute a small drawing to the main chart. Reproduce the chart and send it home. Another

Parent Communication Center

YOU'LL NEED:

one piece of clear vinyl

pencil

32" x 60"

scissors

sewing machine

4' length of string

32" long piece of ½" thick dowel

WHAT TO DO:

1. Cut the piece of vinyl into the following sizes:
- one 40"x31" (hanging)
- three 10½"x 11" pieces
- one 10½ x 9" piece
- two 10½"x 5" pieces

2. Fold all edges of the piece under ½" and sew:

← cut away

3. Fold over the top side (30" side) by 3" and sew across the top to form a pocket for the dowel piece.

4. Sew the vinyl pocket pieces, as shown, onto the large piece ½" in from edge.

5. Patch pockets

6. Tie each end of a 36" piece of string to each end of dowel at top of hanging. Attach pencil with remaining string.

way to use the experience chart is to write it as a group and then attach a copy to a piece of artwork that each child has made during the week.

You will also find that these sheets are helpful reminders and should be kept on file for parent/teacher conferences or for next year's planning. If one child has accomplished something special this week, a short note on her copy of the experience chart is a lovely way of sharing the child's progress in class with her parents.

A TAKE HOME EXPERIENCE CHART

THE FIREHOUSE
This week we went to the firehouse. We made hats like the firemen wore. We collected all the red thi we could f

Please Save/ Scrap Item Box

Reproduce a list of scrap items for parents to save at home rather than discard. Post and pass out this list with items circled that you will be needing for this week's projects. In addition, place a scrap item box near the Communication Center for parents to contribute their throw-aways on a regular basis.

DON'T THROW IT AWAY!

Please save these items. See the many things we can make with them. Place items in our scrap item box. Thanks!

THINGS TO SAVE

- ☐ PAPER ROLLS
- ☐ OATMEAL BOXES
- ☐ MILK CARTONS
- ☐ SHOE BOXES
- ☐ SHEETS
- ☐ ICE CREAM CONTAINERS
- ☐ WOOD SCRAPS
- ☐ JUICE CANS
- ☐ TIN CANS
- ☐ PAPER CLIPS
- ☐ PAPER ROLLS
- ☐ STYROFOAM TRAYS
- ☐ CORKS
- ☐ WALNUT SHELL HALVES
- ☐ SPONGES
- ☐ EGG CARTONS
- ☐ MILK CARTONS
- ☐ EMPTY FOOD CONTAINERS
- ☐ BERRY BASKETS
- ☐ SPICE CANS
- ☐ BOXES
- ☐ PAPER PLATES
- ☐ PAPER CUPS
- ☐ NAPKINS
- ☐ PLASTIC UTENSILS
- ☐ SOCKS
- ☐ NYLON STOCKINGS
- ☐ PAPER MILK CARTONS

THINGS TO MAKE

Paper Rolls Oatmeal Box → ROCKET SHIP

Milk Cartons → PULL TRAIN

Shoe Boxes → DOLL HOUSE ROOMS

Sheets → TENT — GHOST — SLEEPING BAG

Ice Cream Containers → ROBOTS

Wood Scraps → SCULPTURE — ANIMALS — MONSTERS

Juice Cans Tin Cans → TELEPHONE — STOMPERS

Paper Clips → NECKLACE

Paper Rolls → KAZOO — TELESCOPE — MEGAPHONE

Shells, Corks Sponges, trays → BOATS

Egg/Milk Cartons → A CASTLE

Food Containers → A STORE   25¢   50¢   COOKIES

Boxes → CAGE — DOLL BED — HOUSE

Paper Goods → A RESTAURANT

Socks Stockings → SOCK PUPPETS — OLD FACES

Milk Containers → CUT — BLOCKS

Newsletter

A newsletter, which should come out monthly or at least four to six times a year, is useful for keeping parents informed about special activities, trips, and events coming up at school. It can prepare them for what to expect: your need for volunteers and materials and dates to keep open. It's also a good place to share pertinent health and childcare information.

Your newsletter is just that—YOUR newsletter. It is unique to your school, alone. The newsletter is letting parents know that philosophically you want them as educational partners. It demonstrates what you consider important activities and events, so it helps parents to understand your educational philosophy.

The newsletter should make parents feel very much a part of their child's learning and an essential part of the school. It should convey to parents that you care about them and need their help to coordinate and run fundraisers and major events, to locate or donate material goods, or just to be helping hands. The newsletter also gives parents a common ground for talking with each other. They can discuss the class news as they get to know each other better.

It's best to keep your newsletter short—one page—and to the point. Busy parents tend to put lengthy newsletters aside until "later," and then somehow they get lost and are never read.

Have You Seen These?

Very often, notices are never received by parents when they are sent home via the children or the mail. A master sheet with the name of the important notices listed is a good way to make sure that information is received. It's also a good place for parents to check on registration, health forms, and permission slips that you need for each child.

NEWSLETTER

"YOUR NAME" NEWSLETTER

What's Coming Up . . . ?

★ We will be taking a trip to a farm on Friday, Sept. 16th.

★ We will begin to learn colors next week. Red is the first color.

★ Parent-Teacher Coffee Night will be held on Tuesday, October 5th. All are welcome. Come meet other parents!

★ We will be starting a child development course next week on Sept. 8th. Sign Up!

What's Cooking?

To celebrate the fall harvest, we will be making all sorts of apple recipes. We would love to have your child bring in one apple - it can be any color and variety.

We will need parent helpers for our farm trip. We need four parents to drive. If you can help, see Mrs. Horowitz.

We need parents to help with our Halloween Party in October. See sign-up sheet on Communication Board.

Parent Exchange

A few parents on the north section of Main St. would like to form a car pool. Call Mr. Hill.

Help, we need babysitters. If you have any to share. Call Mrs. Faggella.

Book Check Out

You can encourage parents to read to their children with a Parent/Child Pick-a-Book Program. Open your library corner to parents as well as the children. Let them choose a book together and keep it for a week. It might be one of the many books you've recommended to the parent or child, based on your observations of the child's interests. This check-out book list will make it very easy for you to keep track of your books.

Our Trip

Mention where you are going, date, time, and place. Some of the parents might like to join you.

You Are Invited

If a special event is coming up, post your invitation here. (See Chapter Five for special events and creative invitations.)

We Need Your Help

Post a sign-up sheet for the activities that require parental help. (See pages 42-43.)

Parent-to-Parent

Often, parents have found excellent, creative ways of dealing with those everyday situations that all families encounter. A parent-to-parent spot on the bulletin board gives families a lovely way to share this information, as well as a place to ask others for assistance. For example, one part of this spot might be called I NEED HELP FROM OTHER PARENTS. This area can be concerned with car pools, babysitters, and so on.

BOOK CHECK OUT!

1. _____
2. _____
3. _____
4. _____
5. _____
6. _____
7. _____
8. _____
9. _____
10. _____
11. _____
12. _____
13. _____
14. _____
15. _____
16. _____
17. _____

TAKE A BOW

"Give children and parents many opportunities to feel proud."

When a child does something special at school—learns a new skill, is very helpful, shares information, does anything that can be praised—let her family know. The child will feel a tremendous sense of pride thus helping to build up her self-esteem and her parents will feel a pat on the back as well. Parents who are experiencing difficulties with their child especially need to hear as many positive things about her as possible.

There are several ways of getting this information home so that it will be noticed.

■ Keep handy large, sticky, colorful stars. Use them as rewards for positive behavior. Next to the star, mention what the child did that was special. You can stick these right onto the child's clothes or onto any sheet of paper that is going home.

■ Drop a short "thought you'd like to know..." note in the child's lunchbox. The lunchbox is one place that parents are sure to inspect.

"Send home 'special information' in special ways."

■ Pin a badge or certificate on the child's clothes describing how wonderful she has been. You can duplicate and fill in the BADGES and CERTIFICATES on pages 34 and 35.

■ Use large, fancy, colorful safety pins—the ones that children just love to wear—to attach "I'm Special" notes.

■ Make the special "TAKE-HOME" BAGS on the facing page with the children. Personalize each with the child's name and artwork. The bags have a special pocket for parent notices.

■ Send home an audiotape (or video cassette) that a parent and child can listen to together to share activities at school. The child can have the added fun and experience of making these tapes with the teacher's assistance. Sending home a tape is also an excellent way of reaching parents when phone calls or letters have failed. By listening to a tape, parents who resist participation or are too busy to do so, can still feel as though they are connected to their child's school. The child can describe her classroom, some activities, a specific song, or talk about a new skill.

TAKE HOME BAG

YOU'LL NEED:

one brown grocery bag per child

ruler

glue

markers

scissors

WHAT TO DO:

1. Keep bag folded and cut away top portion as shown below.

2. Overlap the "handle pieces" so that each end sets down into the bag about 1". Glue handles together.

3. Glue a piece of cut-off bag (9"×5") onto side as a "patch pocket."

cut away

9"   9"

5"   5"

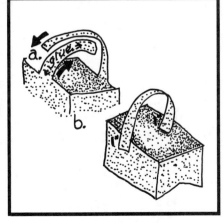
a. glue
b.

Children can decorate with markers.

BADGES

1. Reproduce these badges.

   Color each with markers.

2. Mount and glue this page on cardboard. Let dry.

3. Cut out each badge.

4. Cut two pieces of ribbon. Glue to back of badge.

5. Glue a pin backing onto the back of the badge. Use masking tape instead of backings, if desired!

CERTIFICATES

Seal of Approval

earned by

_____

for _____

signed _____ date _____

DOG GONE IT, ☆ YOU'RE GREAT ☆

earned by

for _____

signed _____ date _____

Just Thought You'd LIKE TO KNOW...

_____

_____

_____

signed _____ date _____

I'M SPECIAL

_____

signed _____ date _____

SUPER WORK

_____

_____

signed _____ date _____

A Whale of a Job!

_____

_____

signed _____ date _____

PARENT/TEACHER MEETINGS

Send home a letter inviting parents to their conference. It's a nice way to let them know some of your feelings about the conference and a good reminder for them of their appointment date and time. A sample letter follows.

Dear Parents:

It's time for our parent/teacher conference.

I'm looking forward to meeting with you since conferences are a good way for us to get to know each other, to share our views of your child, and to help each other with any difficulties.

If there is a specific problem or situation that you'd like to discuss with me, it's best if you could let me know the nature of it beforehand by note, phone, or at pick-up/drop off times. This way, I can spend some time before our meeting thinking about it and making observations of your child.

I will see you at school on the date and time below. Please let me know if your scheduled conference is inconvenient and we will change the time.

Thank you,

Your child's teacher

Our conference is scheduled for _____

PREPARATION

There are several things that you can use at parent/teacher conferences to make them more productive. When you present samples of a child's work and descriptions of her behavior in class, it is easier for parents to understand what and how their child is doing at school.

Artwork

A child's artwork can reveal many of her thoughts and feelings. Ask the child to tell you about a picture when she has completed it. By writing her exact words on the corner or back of the picture, you will be able to recall her ideas and share them with her parents. Parents may not be aware of some of these thoughts and feelings; sharing them can help parents gain a better understanding of their child. The pride and joy that a child's artwork often brings makes it a good place for starting a discussion about the child. You also can talk about the child's style of drawing, her concentration level, the type of strokes that she uses, the materials that she favors, and so on.

Sociogram

This is a chart that shows play and friendship patterns in a class of children. Information is gathered by both observation and direct questioning. Ask each child separately, "With whom do you like to play?" "Who are your best friends?" Compare your observations with the answers children give. You can make two charts. One will reflect the direct answers from children; the other shows the play patterns as you observed them through a few free play periods. Comparisons of the two charts below show the following:

■ Benji is perceived as the "leader" or most popular child. All the children name him as someone they consider a playmate. Actual play patterns, however, show that Benji plays only with Jason and Tony. He teases the girls when they all are in a group, but never seems to relate to Bob or Jeff.

■ The three girls stick closely together. They allow Bob to join in their play frequently, yet they never mention him as a chosen playmate. Bob says Benji is a playmate, as shy children are apt to do with popular children, but he never actually plays with him.

■ Jeff is a loner who constantly seeks out the company of the teachers and other adults

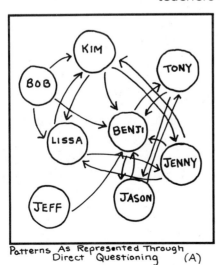

Patterns As Represented Through Direct Questioning (A)

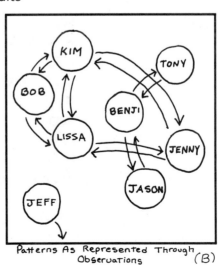

Patterns As Represented Through Observations (B)

Photographs

It's a good idea to snap individual and group shots of children at work and play on a regular basis. Photographs are reminders of things that you've done in class and of children's behavior patterns. They also serve as examples of behaviors you may wish to point out to parents.

Note Cards

You can carry around a small notebook in class to jot down a child's comment or to record behavioral observations. You may want to make notes about the child's level of self-esteem, motivation, and social behavior. It's so easy to forget those daily observations and perceptions that would be helpful to remember at conference time.

CONFERENCE TIME

At a parent/teacher conference, you want to accomplish some of the following:

■ SHARE your observations of the child's consistent behavior and developing patterns, any concerns, and all of the delightful things that you've had the pleasure of noticing

■ EXCHANGE INFORMATION with parents about their child. Conferences are a two-way exchange of information. Find out about the child's behavior at home—general attitudes, activities, interests and behavior, medical needs, and if possible, family stresses, unusual circumstances, or problems that could affect her behavior in school.

■ EXPLORE ways of dealing together with the problems or difficulties each of you might be experiencing. The frustrations and concerns that a parent might be having at home may not be present at school and vice versa. Examine ways that you can support each other and solve problems together.

■ COMPARE the way their child is doing at school with the way they might perceive her. So many parents have been surprised at the differences.

■ CLARIFY expectations. Sharing what you would like to see happen for the child in the near future can help many parents with their own expectation level at home.

■ SUGGEST ways of working with the child at home that have been particularly successful at school and suggest experiences that would be beneficial for her to have more of at home (more cooking, reading aloud, and so on.)

PARENTS AS PARTNERS

PARENTS IN THE CLASSROOM

"Plan so that parents can volunteer for a short period of time."

Making sure that each young child's education is individualized takes time and work. Even with a small child-to-teacher ratio, a teacher can always use an extra pair of hands now and then. Your best source of extra help can come from the parents—they are your most interested, motivated, and capable helpers. They are also a great resource when they share their careers and hobbies with the children. And, parent volunteers can free you to spend more time with individual children.

Plan a schedule so that the parents can volunteer for a few months at a time. This will make it easier for them to make the commitment. Have a coffee or tea to explain the different jobs; point out the sign-up sheets, and answer any questions. Be sure to emphasize the importance of these jobs and that you will be there to help volunteers. Point out that through these experiences, parents, especially young ones, have a chance to develop their parenting skills and can see firsthand ways to help their children learn concepts and skills at home. Later in the year, have another coffee or tea as a "thank you" for a job well done and to make parents feel they have done something really necessary.

You can use the following two "We Need Your Help" forms to organize your volunteer system and to notify parents of how and when they are needed. The shorter form can be filled in and sent home for any of your projects, activities, or events for which you might need some help; for example, "We will be cooking pretzels on...We need assistants..." or "We will be going to the farm on...We need drivers..." The longer form can be posted on the bulletin board for parents to sign. It a general call for volunteers from which you can get helpers for each specific event. (If you need drivers, you can send the short letter home to parents on the larger volunteer list who said that they'd like to be drivers.)

WE'D LIKE YOUR HELP

Dear Parents,

We will be _____

_____ on _____

and would love to have you be a

part of it.

We need _____.

If you can help, let _____

know, as soon as possible.

Thank you for your continuing

cooperation.

_____

Your Child's Teacher

Dear Parents:

We need some of you to help us with the following jobs for the next few months. We'd like at least two people (or more as indicated) to sign up for each job so that you can share the responsibility. Please sign your name and telephone number in the space provided so that we can call you when we need you. Thank you. It's nice to know that you are there to help!

Librarians   Set up and maintain our book corner by getting donations and overseeing the book check-out list.

1. _____   2. _____

Photographers   Take pictures for our class photo album of our work, play, and special events.

1. _____   2. _____

Scrap Material Gatherers   Check out stores and factories for their castoffs and contributions.

PLACE	MATERIAL	USE AT SCHOOL
Lumberyard	wood scraps	sculptures, bookends, boats, trains
name and phone no.		
Ice Cream Store	empty containers	space helmets, waste baskets, storage, and pull toys
name and phone no.		
Appliance Store	boxes	buildings, tunnels, to climb on, in, and over puppet theater
name and phone no.		
Soda Company	wooden crates	tiny shelves and carrying cases
name and phone no.		
Post Office	end of stamp sheets	make our own stamps
name and phone no.		
Print Shop or newspaper factory	scrap paper	drawing, cutting
name and phone no.		

Phone Caller   Set up a network to notify parents of school closings and events.

1. _____   2. _____

Drivers for Trips   (Indicate days available.)

1. _____

2. _____

3. _____

Animal Caretaker   Arrange weekend care for classroom pets with the families. _____

Outdoor Maintenance Helpers   Help keep up our outdoor equipment.

1. _____

2. _____

3. _____

Indoor Maintenance Helpers   Help keep up our indoor equipment.

1. _____

2. _____

3. _____

Snack Makers

1. _____

2. _____

Clean-up Committee   Help us tidy up after the special parent/child events. Hopefully, each parent will have to do it only once.

EVENT	HELPER

Project Assistant   Come volunteer and have a good time helping us do our projects in the following areas:

woodworking _____

cooking _____

arts and crafts _____

Career / Hobby Sharer   During the year, we will be teaching about careers and hobbies. Come in and share yours.

NAME	CAREER OR HOBBY

YOURS FOR THE MAKING

"Build an inexpensive playground with help from parents."

You can build an inexpensive playground with parental help. Building an outside play area requires lots of planning, hard work, adult cooperation, and determination to track down the inexpensive or free materials that are available. But, the result can be terrific.

One daycare center built a fantastic playground using a lot of free materials—tires, telephone poles, dismantled equipment from a previous playground, tree stumps, and hardware. Lumber and sand were their biggest costs. All labor was donated by the Kiwanis Club, parents, and the board of directors. Their project (one large climbing area, a smaller climbing area, and a solar sandbox) took one year to complete on a gradual basis.

An outdoor play area can include:
- water, sand or mud
- climbing equipment
- movable equipment for the children to do their own building
- swings
- covered places to hide

If you're interested in this type of project, visit other playgrounds for ideas and try to talk with the people who were involved.

You can hire an architect to help. If you can't afford one, check with a local college to see if an architecture student (supervised by a professor) would be willing to help out. It is important to have someone who is available familiar with construction. Do you have a parent in construction work?

"The most important consideration is the children's safety."

Remember the most important consideration of all is the children's safety. For example, mats, sand, or some type of soft cushioning material are necessary under all climbing equipment and slides. All the wood pieces need to be well sanded and smooth and there should be no sharp edges on any equipment.

You can find many inexpensive materials around your community. In some places, you can get these things free. Be resourceful. Look for the items at the places in parentheses on the following page that can be made into playground equipment.

Once built, a playground needs continued involvement and interest in its maintenance. Watch over it and use it. The playground needs to be checked on a regular basis to make sure that all nuts and bolts are secure. Be sure to put up a sign that says, "This playground was built by _____. Please take good care of it."

PLAYGROUND

BARRELS
for houses, Climbing
and tunnels
(from garden shops,
brewery, wineries)

SODA
CRATES
for building
(from bottler)

TIRE
SWING

PLASTIC SHOWER
CURTAIN
for Teepees, slippery slide
(from home, neighbors)

CARGO NET
for climbing

OLD ROWBOAT
for pretend
(from boat yard)

BRICKS
for building
(from lumber yard)

RAILROAD TIES
for sand box, balance beam,
construction
(from lumber yards)

TIRES
for swings, obstacle course, Tunnels
(from local garage, tire store)

ROCKS
for stepping stones
(from garden shops,
gardens, woods)

SPOOLS
for Table, chairs
(from utility companies,
cable T.V.)

GARDENING

"Start your parent/child gardening project in the late spring."

Plan a cooperative parent/child gardening project in the late spring and you will have plenty of opportunities for gathering families together during the summer and into the early fall.

The major ingredient in gardening is patience. It takes time to grow seeds into seedlings, then into plants, and finally into the ready-to-be harvested fruits and vegetables. However, the process is constantly filled with amazing progress that is fun for both children and adults to watch.

You will need a small plot of land. If you are fortunate enough to have school property, find a sunny, lightly trafficked area. All it takes is a 10' x 15' or 20' plot for a great, kid–sized harvest. If you do not have land of your own, see if you can plant a garden at a senior citizen's home, nursing home, or community center.

Announce the garden plans to parents and children. You might bring in a variety of vegetables to show the children that these are some of the ones that they can grow in their garden. Take a poll and see which are the favorites and be sure to try to include those. Ask for help from the parents, perhaps on a late weekday afternoon or a Saturday morning, to come up and till the soil. Parents and children can bring shovels to turn it over. Add a couple of bags of processed sheep or cow manure and peat moss for denser soils. You will find that the plants will respond better to this richer and lighter soil. When the soil is ready, adults and children can plan the rows by marking them with some string and a few sticks to make sure they will be straight. (Remember to plant the rows east to west to follow the course of the daily sun. In this way, each row gets the sun and taller plants do not block the sun as they would in a garden planted with north to south rows.)

"Let each family contribute a few plants or seeds."

Each family might like to bring in a few plants or seeds. Be sure to include lettuce, tomato, radish, green beans, carrot, squash, cucumber, and flowers like marigolds. Check a gardening book for special instructions for the more unusual plants you might choose. Plant seeds according to package directions and transplant seedlings carefully.

Children can take over the watering each day. Set up a cabinet or shelf with watering cans so children have easy access to them. Help the children keep a gardening journal by recording the weather—in pictures—and temperature each day and measuring plant growth once a week with a ruler. Include drawings of all the plants at various stages. Parents can help by occasionally cultivating the soil, showing the children how to keep the garden weed free, and tying up the taller plants during the summer.

During the summer, pick the lettuce, radishes, and green beans for added vegetables at lunchtime. In late summer, harvest the tomatoes and other slower growing vegetables. Parents and children can share a lunch with all the produce. Save a few vegetables by pickling the cucumbers, putting the squash into cold storage, and freezing made-ahead dishes of vegetables. It will be fun to share the garden's bounty in the middle of winter!

The excitement of the garden sustains itself with each new fruit or vegetable produced. Parents and children are sharing a wonderful experience. You are the catalyst for not only the hands-on experience of gardening and witnessing of the cycle of nature, but also for bringing parents and children together.

"Have a special parent/child lunch featuring produce from the garden."

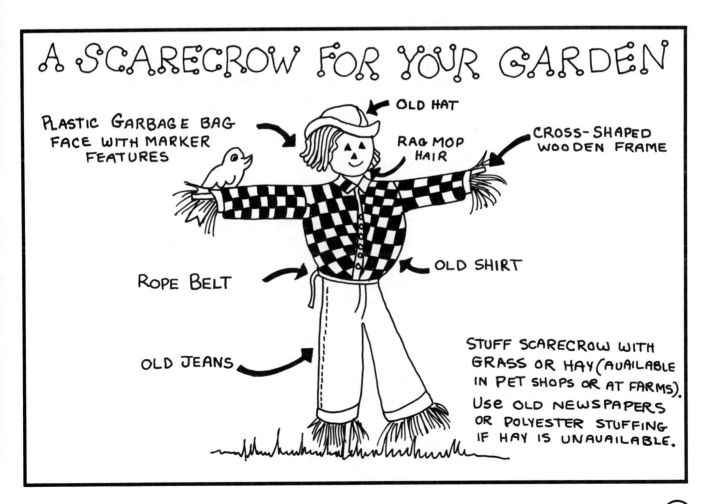

A SCARECROW FOR YOUR GARDEN

PLASTIC GARBAGE BAG FACE WITH MARKER FEATURES

OLD HAT

RAG MOP HAIR

CROSS-SHAPED WOODEN FRAME

OLD SHIRT

ROPE BELT

OLD JEANS

STUFF SCARECROW WITH GRASS OR HAY (AVAILABLE IN PET SHOPS OR AT FARMS). USE OLD NEWSPAPERS OR POLYESTER STUFFING IF HAY IS UNAVAILABLE.

GIFT-MAKING WORKSHOPS

Parents and children can come together in a creative series of workshops to make crafty gifts that can be taken home or sold at a class or school craft fair. It is best to schedule this activity around a holiday season. Workshops can be scheduled during the regular arts/crafts period for each classroom. Parents can volunteer to come in for one hour whenever the class is working on the gifts. Have a sign-up sheet for the volunteers to choose the time, the day, and the project that most interests them.

An alternative suggestion—one that takes more coordination, yet is also more fun—is to set aside one or possibly two days for all the children to come to a special workshop. To run this one or two-day, gift-making workshop, you'll need parent volunteers, materials, poster-sized directions (See ideas on pages 50-57.), and a good schedule. Send out a "call for help" to parents and have a planning meeting at which you show the parents the gift choices and discuss exactly what they will be doing. Tell them that they need volunteer for only one hour which would include preparation time, 20-30 minutes working with the children and 15 minutes for clean up. Have a sign-up sheet available to schedule these one hour time slots. Schedule several parents to work at the same time, if space permits. (Parents like working together.) You might also ask parents to help collect materials for the workshop at the meeting. Pass out a list of things you'll need and make sure every item is covered. The school will probably have to provide the glue, scissors, markers, and some paper.

Some gifts will require purchased materials; therefore you will have to consider how to cover the costs these gifts require. The cost of the materials and equipment could be covered in one of three ways: by the school as part of the art budget, by each child who could be charged $.50 per craft (collected in advance), or by the parent volunteer who provides and donates the materials for a gift on which she has chosen to work.

At the time of the actual workshop, you must coordinate the whole effort. You can set up a table in a corner or use a whole room for the workshop. Make or reproduce the posters with directions and hang over a table with the materials needed for that specific craft. This makes it easier for each new parent volunteer not only to have the specific directions on how to do the craft, but also to have the materials right at hand.

Each child chooses a gift to make. Then, you bring the children

"Encourage parents to come into school for an hour to help children make gifts for the holidays."

to the parent and introduce them. The child and parent volunteer spend about 20-30 minutes working on the project. Be sure to show the parents where these "objects d'art" can be safely placed to dry or, when completed, to be stored until they can be gift-wrapped and sent home or sold. Clearly mark trash cans for easy parent and child cleanup. The parent is responsible for putting away materials so the next volunteer can easily find them.

These gift-making workshops, particularly when done in one or two days, are lively and filled with a sense of the holiday spirit. It is lovely to see the generous help provided by parents and even grandparents, who often come in to help just for an hour and end up staying all day! Their enthusiasm spreads to the children, making it an exciting time for everyone.

CRAFT SALE

The craft gifts produced during these workshops also could be used at your very own class craft show and sale. This creates a fun, mini-economics lesson for the children.

"A craft sale is also an economics lesson for young children."

As a class, decide what you'd like to buy to add to the classroom: a new book to read, a record, more blocks, or toy cars. Discuss the fact that it takes money to buy something new and that the class will have to earn this money. Suggest things that the children could make to sell at your class' craft sale. Ask children if they have any old toys that they would be willing to donate to the craft sale to put on the "White Elephant" table. (Don't expect too much from this. Children seem to have a difficult time parting with old toys, even the ones they never play with.)

Invite the parents to the craft show which could be held 15-20 minutes before dismissal one day. The children can walk around the craft show with their parents and "shop." All the items should be priced very inexpensively so that there is no monetary pressure on the parents.

After the sale, have the children help you count the money. They can sort the different coins and bills. Then, take a class trip to a local store to purchase the item that the class has chosen.

Love Bug Bookmark

YOU'LL NEED:

cardboard or posterboard

red/black markers

photo(s) of child

scissors

red yarn

pencil

glue

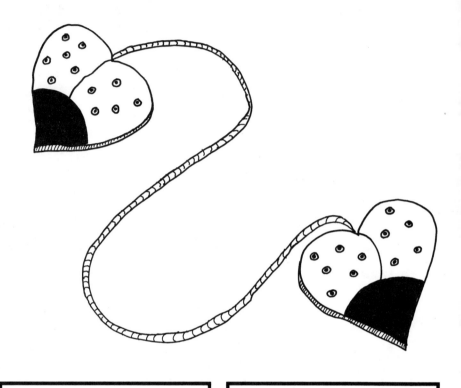

WHAT TO DO:

1. Make a heart pattern by placing thumb over fold on a piece of folded paper.

← Adult Thumb

2. Use heart pattern and trace four hearts onto cardboard or posterboard. Child or adult cuts them out.

3. Sandwich one end of yarn between two hearts and glue. Repeat for other end.

4. Let both hearts dry under a stack of books.

5. Use markers to decorate hearts like "lady bugs".

6. Glue small photo(s) to back side(s) of each heart.

BOOKENDS

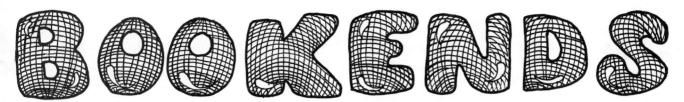

YOU'LL NEED:

 two quart or half gallon milk cartons

 scissors

 plasticene clay

glue

 2 large rocks

 shells

 craft knife

plaster of paris

scrap felt pieces

WHAT TO DO:

1. Adults cuts the two milk cartons in half.

2. Adult cuts each bottom half of the milk carton on the diagonal.

DISCARD

SAVE

3. Tilt the bottom piece so that the open side is up. Prop it in place using clay. Now, fill with prepared plaster of paris.

CLAY   CLAY

4. While plaster of paris is still wet, insert rock, shells so that they show on top of the plaster of paris. Let dry. Tear away carton.

ROCK

SHELLS

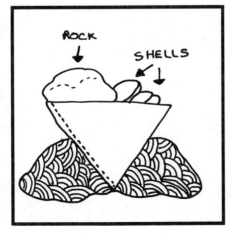

5. Glue felt to bottom.

FELT

NECKTIE DRAFT CATCHER

YOU'LL NEED:

 old necktie (wide ones are best)

 Sand

 funnel

 scissors

tacky glue

red felt scrap

 moveable craft eyes

needle and thread

WHAT TO DO:

1. Adult or child sews one end of tie closed. Use a very tight stitch.

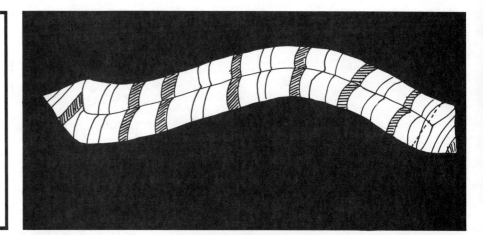

2. Child can use funnel to fill tie snake with sand.

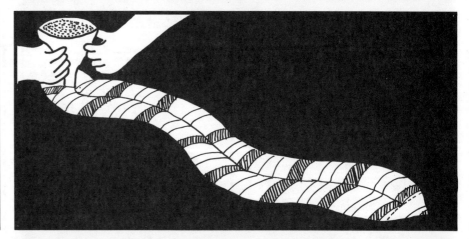

3. Child or adult sew 'head' end of tie tightly closed. Use glue to attach eyes. Cut out and glue on scrap felt tongue.

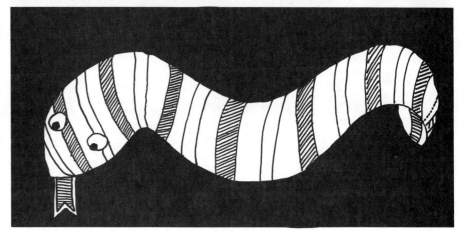

TIE AND JEWELRY HOLDER

YOU'LL NEED:

 a long, 3/4" thick piece of soft wood, such as pine

large headed nails

 cup hooks

permanent markers

hammer

WHAT TO DO:

1. With nails and hammer, child puts four or five "hooks" into the wood for a tie hanger.

2. To make a jewelry hanger, use the nails to start the holes, then screw in cup hooks.

3. Decorate the wood with markers. Use more nails to hang.

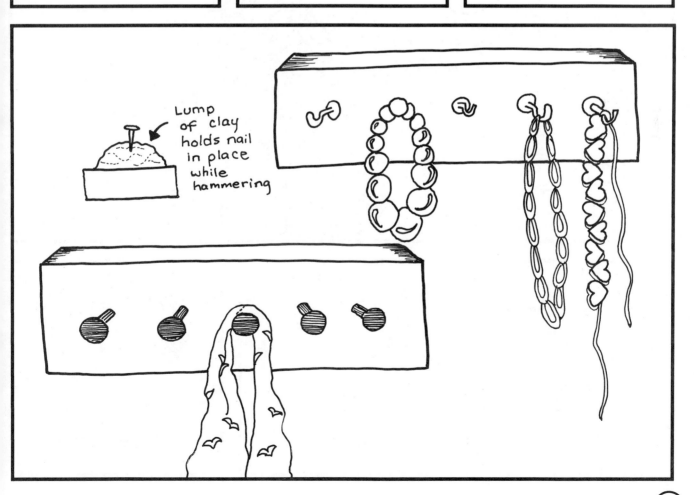

Lump of clay holds nail in place while hammering

53

A HOLIDAY TREE

YOU'LL NEED:

a cone-shaped ice cream cone

½ cup margarine
2 cups confectionary sugar
2 tsp. milk
green food color

trims (mini-marshmallows, red hots, chocolate chips, raisins

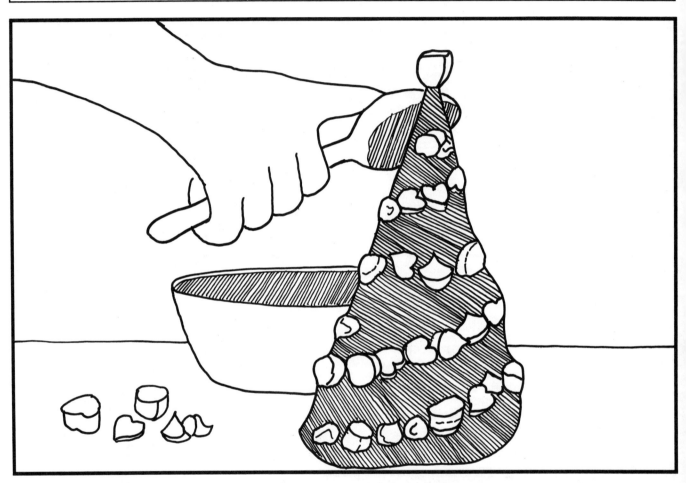

WHAT TO DO:

1. Combine sugar, margarine, and milk in a bowl. Blend well. Add food color to tint green.

2. Cover the cone with green frosting.

3. Use trims to decorate the "tree." This craft gift makes a great centerpiece.

HOLIDAY ORNAMENTS

YOU'LL NEED:

white yarn

Waxed paper
white glue

sweetheart sugar cones

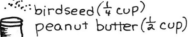
birdseed (¼ cup)
peanut butter (½ cup)
bacon drippings (2 tbsp.)
ribbon

various shaped pretzels

1 egg white

1 cup confectionary sugar

WHAT TO DO:

1 SPIDER WEBS

Place glue in a wide, flat container. Cut yarn into 8"-10" lengths. Children dip strings, one at a time, into glue, covering them thoroughly.

Place string pieces on waxed paper, crossing each at the center to make a multi pointed star effect.

Children dip one 18" length into glue and then spiral it around the star-shaped pieces. Let dry overnight. Peel off waxed paper and tie a string on to hang.

2 BIRDFEEDER CONES

Mix together peanut butter, bacon drippings and birdseed. Stuff mixture into cone.

Tie a ribbon around cone and make a loop on the cone to hang it from outside tree branches.

Variation: Fill cone with candies, wrap in red netting, secure with velvet ribbon.

3 PRETZEL PRIZES

Whip one egg white until foamy. Add confectionary sugar. (Keep mixture covered so sugar will stay soft and slightly runny.)

Place pretzels, in a design shape, on waxed paper. Use egg-sugar 'glue' to attach pieces together. Let dry overnight. Remove from wax paper. Tie a piece of yarn on pretzel prize to hang.

FAMILY SCRAPBOOK

YOU'LL NEED:

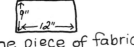
one piece of fabric

 five sheets of 8½" x 11" typing paper

hole puncher

pinking shears

yarn needle

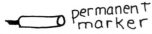 yarn

permanent marker

WHAT TO DO:

 1. Fold sheets of paper in half to make each page 8½" tall and 5½" wide. Fold fabric in half to make each cover 9" x 6".

 2. Adult punches two holes in folded paper pages about ½" from fold and about 4" apart. Use scissors to cut similar holes in fabric cover.

 3. Adult threads needle and child sews yarn through cover and paper pages, then ends are tied in a bow.

 4. Child or adult uses permanent markers to write child's name and the year on the cover.

 5. Have child name each person in her family. Place one name on each double page.

 6. Child can illustrate that family member and draw favorite things. You can take dictated stories, type them and add to scrapbook.

A PLAY~CLAY PENCIL HOLDER

YOU'LL NEED:

1 cup baking soda

½ cup cornstarch

¾ cup water

food colors
markers
pencils
saucepan

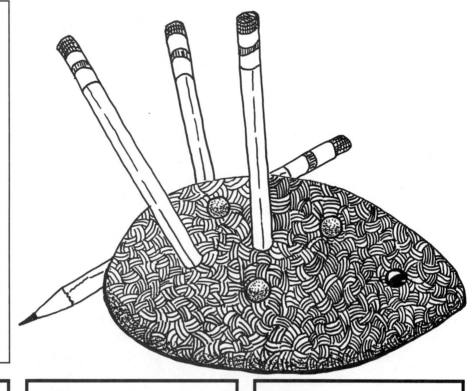

WHAT TO DO:

1. Mix baking soda and cornstarch in a saucepan. Add ten drops of any color food color with water and add both to contents in saucepan.

2. Adult cooks, slowly, the contents on medium heat until it thickens and resembles mashed potatoes. Cool slightly.

3. Knead a lump of play clay and then shape it into a mound so it looks like a porcupine.

4. Use a pencil to poke holes into the porcupine's back. Poke two shallow holes for eyes.

5. Allow the pencil holder porcupine to dry for a day or two.

6. Use the markers to put designs and names all over porcupine pencil holder.

WANTED: WORKING PARENTS

"Parents are a terrific resource for a unit on careers."

"Sometimes, you can plan a field trip to a parent's place of work."

During the preschool years, children like to imitate their parents. So parents make an excellent resource for a unit on careers.

Having them share their careers in the classroom is a nice, easy way of encouraging parents to contribute to and be part of their child's early learning experience. Children can easily relate to and feel comfortable with adults who are related to their classmates.

To get this program going, send home a JOB QUESTIONNAIRE for parents to discuss and fill out with their children. When a parent expresses an interest in sharing his job with your class, set up a specific date and time to coordinate with your teaching theme. Be sure that you give the parent enough advance notice so that he can make the necessary arrangements.

If a parent's work environment is very unusual or such that the parent cannot come into school to share it with the children, an excursion to his work place would make a wonderful field trip. (A pilot might be able to show the children the inside of a small airplane and the control room; a veterinarian could let the children tour the animal hospital and take a quick peak at the recuperating pets.) Keeping the visit short and having the children well prepared will help to make your trip a success. One parent who works in a busy office was able to arrange for a short visit of his child's class during the lunch hour. The children were able to compare the work in that office to their "work" in their own classroom. When they returned to class, their activities involved general office supplies. They made paper clip necklaces, label pictures (They drew and colored the blank, sticky labels.), and rubber stamp pictures. They were able to imitate "office workers" by playing in the mini-office area set up (with supplies and a toy or broken typewriter) in a corner of the room.

When parents come into school to share their careers, suggest that they wear their uniform (if they have one), bring in special tools or equipment, and plan to show children how they do a part of their work. For example, a beautician may want to trim his child's hair; a doctor may want to let children listen to heartbeats through a stethoscope; a salesperson might demonstrate the products that are sold. When a working parent visits the school, make sure that lots of pictures are taken. Use these in CAREER BOOKS described on page 60.

You also can provide follow-up experiences based on the visit. For example, after a sculptor or builder's visit, allow the children to use similar tools (hammer, nails) and materials (glue, wood) to make wood sculptures. Whatever type of work or hobby a parent shares, it is best if it can be followed up with activities and enough materials for the children to role play the person who visited.

Job Questionnaire

Dear Parents:

   We will be discussing careers next week and your child will be telling us about what you do. So, please use the questionnaire below to discuss your job with your child. (Remember, homemaking is an important career!) Then, fill it out and have your child return it to school. We hope that you will be able to join us to share your job and/or hobby some time this year. Thank you for your help.

Name (of parent) _____

Address _____

Telephone No. _____

Where do you work? _____

What are your responsibilities? _____
_____

What is your favorite part of the job? _____
_____

Could our class visit the place where you work? _____
_____

What are your hobbies? _____

Would you be willing to share your work or hobby with the other children in our class? _____

What day of the week and time would be most convenient for you to visit? _____

BOOK OF CAREERS

YOU'LL NEED:

 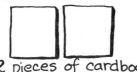
2 pieces of cardboard
(9" high by 6" wide)

12 pieces of paper
(8½" X 11")

needle and strong thread

glue

ruler

plastic tape

WHAT TO DO:

1. Adult folds papers in half and uses needle and thread to sew pages together

2. Make 3 holes in fold and sew: down center hole, up through top hole, back down and through bottom hole. Up again through center hole. Knot.

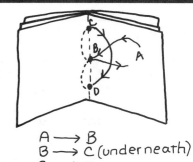
A → B
B → C (underneath)
C → D
D → B (underneath)
2 Knots–very tight

3. Decorate the two pieces of cardboard with pretty papers. Glue papers on and overlap excess to back of cardboard.

4. Glue cardboard covers to front and back of pages. Leave ½" of folded side of pages sticking out.

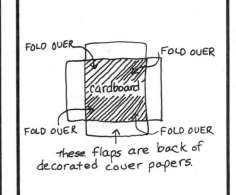
FOLD OVER   FOLD OVER
cardboard
FOLD OVER   FOLD OVER
these flaps are back of decorated cover papers.

5. Place a piece of plastic tape along edge that is sticking out. Fold around to back cover.

6. Open book. Tuck tape ends into book. Tape ends should go under pages.

 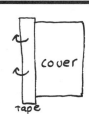
cover

folded side
¼"

cover

tape

☆ Use photos of visitors, cut-outs of people at their places of work, children's illustrations, any any small artifacts.

BIRTHDAYS IN SCHOOL

Children's birthdays are something that all schools have to deal with. In some places, birthdays are handled individually—the parents come to school with treats for everyone in the class. In other centers and schools, one day of each month all children with birthdays in that month are acknowledged with a special celebration, and then the entire class sings "Happy Birthday" to that group.

Whatever your school policy is, make sure that it is clear to all parents. Since most parents are still anxious to do something special on "that date," consider some of the following sugggestions.

Birthday Games

Suggest that parents come into school with one birthday game planned that they will teach to the children in the class. A small snack could also be given at the end of the activity. Ideas for group games can be found in any of the following books in a local library: *Great Parties for Young Children* by Cheryl Barron and Cathy Scherzer; *How to Give a Party* by Jean and Paul Frame; *The Party Book* by Bernice Wells Carlson; *Happy Birthday Parties* by Penny Warner; *Birthday Parties around the World* by Barbara Rinoff.

Healthy Snacks

Parents can cook a healthy birthday treat with the children in the class for all to enjoy together (See page 62 for some suggestions.) Or, parents can prepare individual food kits in plastic bags at home and then send them into school for the children to assemble and then eat.

Birthday Book

Let parents know that they can make a lovely contribution to the school by purchasing a book for the class library in honor of their child's birthday. The book could be any favorite, new, or popular book, or one related to birthdays. The parent can read it to the class and let the "birthday" child talk about it. Birthday book donations—inscribed, of course—are a lovely way to build up a class library.

By encouraging parents to participate in a school activity with their child on the child's birthday, you are helping them share the birthday excitement and make a lovely contribution to the class as well.

Healthy Party Foods

YOU'LL NEED:
cottage cheese
raisins
peanut butter
cereal
popcorn
cheese
pretzels
6oz. chocolate chips
banana
seltzer/club soda
purple cow {
2 cups ice cream
1 cup milk
1 6 oz. can grape juice
}
ice cream
orange
juices =

WHAT TO DO:

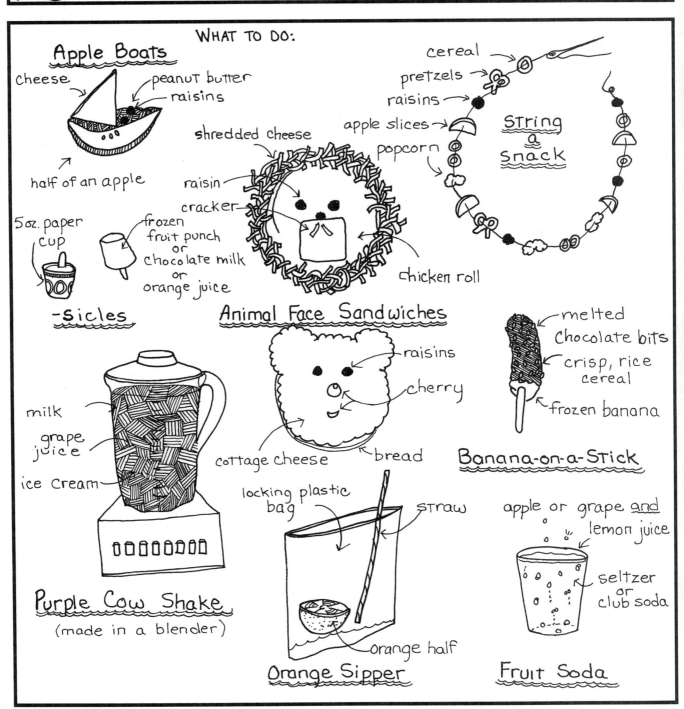

Apple Boats
cheese
peanut butter
raisins
half of an apple

cereal
pretzels
raisins
apple slices
popcorn

String a Snack

shredded cheese
raisin
cracker
chicken roll

5oz. paper cup
frozen fruit punch or chocolate milk or orange juice

-Sicles

Animal Face Sandwiches
raisins
cherry
cottage cheese
bread
locking plastic bag
straw
orange half

Orange Sipper

milk
grape juice
ice cream

Purple Cow Shake
(made in a blender)

melted chocolate bits
crisp, rice cereal
frozen banana

Banana-on-a-Stick

apple or grape and lemon juice
seltzer or club soda

Fruit Soda

SPECIAL EVENTS

EVENTS IN SCHOOL

Inviting parents into your classroom for special events is an exciting time for everyone concerned. Here is one parent's comments to the teacher about her class visit.

"My four year old was so excited about our visit to her classroom that she constantly kept asking us, 'When are you coming into school, Mommy? How many more days? Tell me; count it! Show me on the calendar.'

And, her enthusiasm continued straight through the class' potluck supper. That night, she excitedly pointed out the salad that her class had been preparing for this special occasion. She couldn't wait to show us her projects all around the room and her favorite equipment. She wanted to show off her sister and brother (the whole family was invited) and introduce us to all of her friends. It was also a pleasant, informal way for me to meet the other parents, so that I know who I'm talking to on the telephone when I'm arranging dates.

We all thoroughly enjoyed the experience. It was a lovely thing for us to share and we are looking forward to our next visit. Thank you for making it happen."

"Special events at school can include the whole family."

Special school events that include parents can provide children with many learning experiences. They teach children how to plan, organize, prepare, and wait for the big event to occur. When you are considering the schedule of special events for the year, we suggest the following: start out with the POT LUCK MEAL since it is a good way to help parents meet and socialize with one another. HALLOWEEN will follow at the end of October. January or February is a good time to be indoors for a MUSICAL CONCERT. The UPSIDE DOWN NIGHT could be held in March and be followed by the GAME PARTY in April when the weather starts to warm up. It's best to have the INFORMAL PERFORMANCES toward the end of the year (May or June) as an end-of-the-year party.

"Schedule events throughout the school year."

Discuss the upcoming event with the children in class before sending the invitations home to their parents. Let the children draw or paint a picture or make a collage that you can staple to the invitation that you've copied from this book. It's important for the children to be enthusiastic and excited about bringing these invitations home. They, in effect, are part of the invitation; their enthusiasm and involvement will bring their parents to school.

AN INVITATION

Come Join Us
For A

POT LUCK SUPPER

Date _____
Time _____
What to Bring _____

We will attend _____
We will bring _____

Return this to school.

THE POTLUCK MEAL

The potluck meal, where each family brings in a dish for everyone to share, is a lovely social event to have early in the year. Ask each family to bring in one main dish and have the class provide the rest—dessert and drinks. The abundance of good food encourages conversation among the families, as people share their recipes with young children. This event is a relaxed way for parents to get to know one another and a nice time for the children to begin showing off their room and projects.

PREPARATION

If possible, time your potluck meal so that it comes at the end of a unit on good food and nutrition. Then, encourage the children to talk to their parents about what dish they might like to bring in.

Invitations

The children can make a drawing that you paste on the invitation form found on page 65. In case some parents have trouble deciding what to bring, you can help them by suggesting the following: a pasta, rice, lentil, or potato salad; lasagne; a noodle, chili, or chicken casserole.

Class Recipe Book (optional)

Send home the letter on page 72 requesting one or two favorite family recipes to put into a class book that can be distributed to each family at the end of the meal.

Placemats

Have the children make placemats for themselves and their parents. (See page 70 for ideas.)

Paper Flowers

These can be used as table decorations and then taken home as a souvenir at the end of the meal. (See page 71 for directions.)

On the day of the potluck meal, let the children set the table and prepare something to be served: a big tossed vegetable or fruit salad, cookies, cake, or muffins for dessert. Whichever you choose, let the children do the washing, peeling, cutting, mixing, and tossing as needed. Set the food up buffet style and let the children serve their parents the meal.

**Invite a Letter to Lunch/
The Alphabet Buffet**

VARIATIONS

Each child's family is assigned a letter and they have to bring in something that either begins with that letter (A=Apples, B=bananas, C=chicken, and so on) or something in the shape of that letter (X-shaped pretzels or a Z-shaped cake). Then, everyone gets to guess the family's letter. To find 26 families, you may have to combine two classes for this.

An Ethnic Meal

Each family brings in a dish typical of their heritage.

Potluck Breakfast

It's a lovely way to start the day. Simply substitute appropriate foods.

**Mother's Day/Father's Day
Celebration**

A special Mother's or Father's Day luncheon is a very special celebration for children and their parents. If parents are advised of the date and time well in advance of this special event, they will make sure that they can attend this luncheon. For the child whose parent cannot attend, arrange to have a substitute "parent"—grandparent, aunt, cousin, or family friend—act as parent for the day. Explain to the child that she will be able to celebrate with her mom or dad at home.

Your children can make flower pots with the invitation taped to the bottom of the pot. Use a styrofoam egg carton flower, a pipe cleaner stem, and some clay to anchor it into a sturdy plastic cup.

The children also can make placemats and placecards and assemble place settings for this very special occasion. Each child can wrap a plastic fork, knife, and spoon in a big, colorful napkin which you can tie with yarn. Placecards can be made from construction paper printed with colorful names and decorated by the children.

On the day of your celebration, welcome the guests of honor with a song. Then, have children lead their parents to the table. If you don't want to ask parents to contribute a main dish for this occasion, simply turn a childmade tossed vegetable salad into a chef's salad by adding cheese and chicken chunks. Have the children bring in rolls or loaves of bread.

For your children, this celebration and the other inschool meals mean lots of work, fun, learning, and a great sense of accomplishment.

EGG·IN·A·BISCUIT

YOU'LL NEED:

 $2\frac{1}{4}$ cups biscuit mix

 $\frac{2}{3}$ cup milk

 10 eggs

1 cup shredded cheese

 rolling pin

 muffin tin

2" cookie cutter

WHAT TO DO:

 1. Mix biscuit mix and milk together in a bowl. Dough should be stiff enough to handle.

 2. Knead dough 10 times. Roll to $\frac{1}{2}$" thick. Cut out each biscuit with cutter.

 3. Press each biscuit round into a section of a muffin tin, shaping it up the sides with a center well.

 4. Break an egg into each biscuit well.

 5. Bake in 400°F oven for 10-15 minutes.

 6. Sprinkle with shredded cheese as egg-in-a-biscuit is removed from oven.

SUPER SALAD

YOU'LL NEED:

green or red leaf lettuce

small can kidney beans or chick peas

½ cup shredded mild cheddar cheese

1 cup Italian salad dressing

tomato broccoli cucumber celery
croutons sunflower seeds

WHAT TO DO:

1. Place beans in a bowl. Add ½ cup Italian dressing to them and set aside for one hour.

2. Wash salad greens, tear into bite-sized pieces. Add to large bowl. Add:

3. top with ½ cup dressing and shredded cheese. Toss lightly. Top with sunflower seeds.

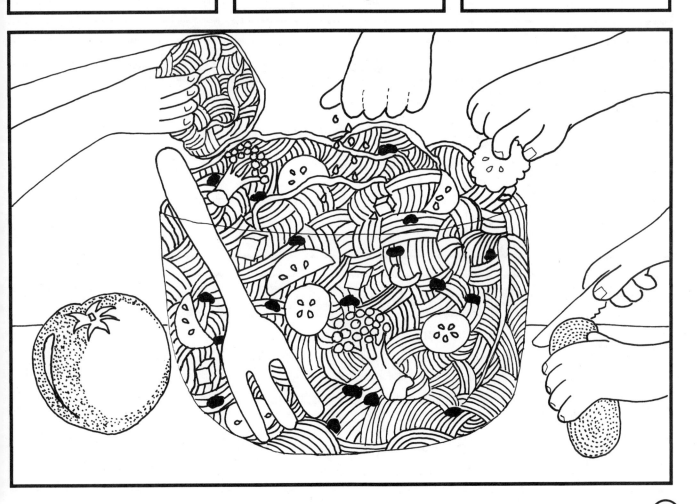

PLACEMATS

YOU'LL NEED:

butcher or shelf paper

clear contact paper

9"x12" white, red, & pink construction paper

markers and crayons

scissors

red (18"x12") construction paper

glue

WHAT TO DO:

1. THE EVER READY RUNNER

1. Let each child design and color one section of a long strip of butcher or shelf paper.
2. Place "runner" on a long table or floor, still intact.

2. THE HARDY-ART PLACEMAT

1. Children draw one large piece of artwork or glue together a collage of art.

2. Place a piece of self-sticking, clear contact paper over artwork.

3. THE PLACE-IN-THE-HEART MAT

1. Fold red paper in half (9"x12")
2. Draw or trace a half heart shape on fold. Cut out.
3. Keep heart folded, cut 6-8 slits into the side with the fold.
4. Cut 12" long by ¾" wide strips of pink and white construction paper.
5. Open up heart and weave strips through slits.
6. Trim strips and dab glue onto a few places to hold strips.

Fantasy Flowers

You'll Need:

pipecleaners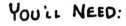

 aluminum foil

colored tissue paper

plastic straws

tape

scissors

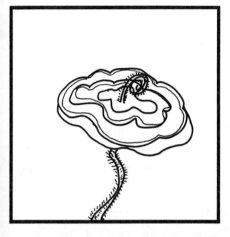

Pipe Cleaner Posies

1.
1. Children slip tissue paper circles over one end of a fuzzy pipe cleaner.

2. Place many layers of paper down about 1".

3. Bend pipe cleaner tip into curliques to hold circles in place.

4. Ruffle paper edges.

Foil Daisies

2.
1. Fold a 10"-12" long piece of aluminum foil in half.

2. Cut scallop edges along the side opposite fold.

3. Gently bunch up fold and tape flower around a drinking straw stem.

Tissue Paper Pompoms

3.
1. Cut several layers of tissue paper 8" long by 4" wide.

2. Use scissors to fringe both sides.

3. Bunch up the paper starting at short ends

4. Tape center of flower around pipe cleaner.

71

CLASS RECIPE BOOK

"Create a recipe book with contributions from each family."

Ask each family to contribute one or two favorite family recipes to put into your class recipe book, preferably the recipes for the food served at your potluck meal. If the class is ethnically mixed, a book of ethnic holiday specialities would be lovely to have—Hungarian pastries, Scandinavian cookies, Italian sweetbread, or Mexican buñuelos. Each recipe can be titled with the child's name, *"Ian's Gingerbread House"* or *"Marta's Butter Cookies."* The children will love seeing their names in the booklet.

Type out each recipe on one page. Photocopy the number needed and staple or bind with yarn. You may wish to give the books to the families at the end of the potluck meal or as holiday gifts. You could charge for them as a fundraiser.

To get things rolling, send home a form for each family to send back. If you are planning to use the recipe book as a fundraiser, put information in the letter about the price and what the money earned will be used for.

Dear Parents:

Our class is creating a Class Recipe Book (8½" x 11" paper) with favorite recipes from each child's family. We would love to have you share one or two of your favorites with us. We would particularly love one of those long-treasured recipes handed down from your parents. Use the space on this sheet to write in the recipe. Return it to us to make our book.

RECIPE

_____

_____

_____

_____

_____

Your name _____

We'd like to use your child's name in the title of the recipe ("Sue's Christmas Quiche"). May we do that? _____

HALLOWEEN PARTY INVITATION

Assemble these special invitations at school and send them home for parents and children to read and do together.

 1. Children tear ghost shapes from white construction paper.

 2. Adult makes copies of invitations on typing weight paper. Make a sandwich by placing the torn paper ghosts between the invitation page and another plain piece of paper.

A.

B.

C.

 3. Glue the two pieces of paper together around <u>edges</u> <u>only</u>.

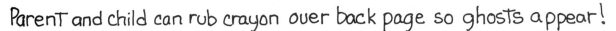 Parent and child can rub crayon over back page so ghosts appear!

HALLOWEEN PARTY

"My daughter was so excited about having us come to the class Halloween party that I thought she would bust. Does she always have so much fun at school? I must admit, I, too, enjoyed playing the games with her. I felt like a kid again as we giggled together. Thank you for having such a good idea at the right time of the year!"

Halloween is the perfect time to have a family party at school. By gathering all the children and parents together, you can eliminate many of the dangers that are associated with this holiday. The party eliminates the discomfort many parents feel about taking their children out trick-or-treating and Halloween, with its traditional use of costumes and treats, lends itself to many fun activities. Most young children will forego the trick-or-treat aspect of Halloween if they know that they will still get to wear make-up, costumes, and have some "treats" at the party. Be sure to take pictures of each child in costume. The pictures will make a lovely, scary class book to keep in your library corner.

PREPARATIONS

Costumes

Make some of the costumes on the facing page with your children or reproduce the page and send it home for parents.

Parents probably should NOT wear costumes as children are often frightened by the sudden change in the people they know and trust. But children can make a paper plate and stick mask for their parent(s) to hold up in front of their faces during the party. Staple or tape a tongue depressor to a paper plate. You must cut out two eye holes. Have children draw a face on plate and then present masks to parents as they come into the party.

Decorations

Make a scary mural by covering one of the walls with drawing paper. Let the children draw their scariest pictures all over it.

Treats

You might want to suggest that parents bring in one small inexpensive grab bag gift for the children. Either you or the parents can provide candy treats or alternatives such as boxes of raisins, yogurt-covered raisins, cracker and peanut butter packages, granola bars, fruit leathers, bags of peanuts, or sunflower seeds.

COSTUMES

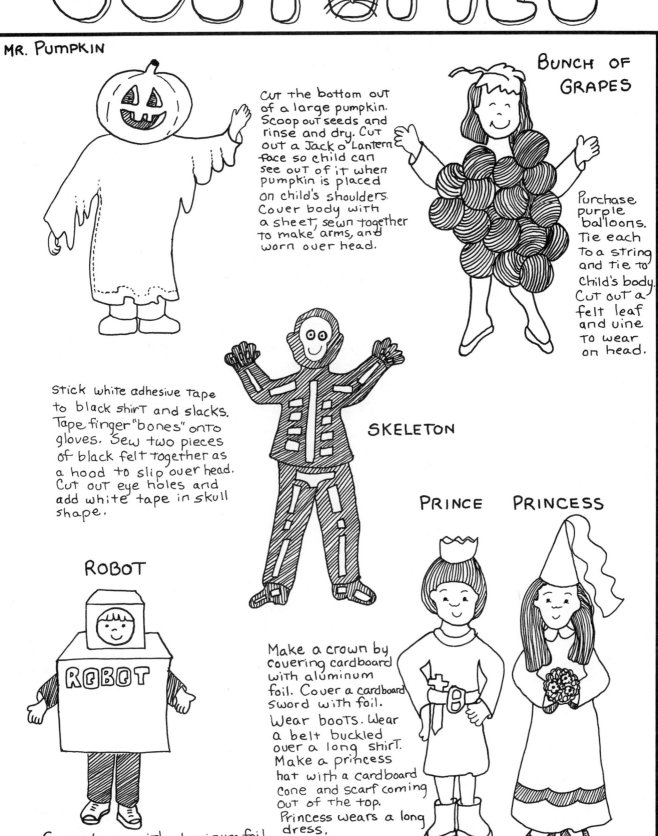

MR. PUMPKIN

Cut the bottom out of a large pumpkin. Scoop out seeds and rinse and dry. Cut out a Jack o' Lantern face so child can see out of it when pumpkin is placed on child's shoulders. Cover body with a sheet, sewn together to make arms, and worn over head.

BUNCH OF GRAPES

Purchase purple balloons. Tie each to a string and tie to child's body. Cut out a felt leaf and vine to wear on head.

Stick white adhesive tape to black shirt and slacks. Tape finger "bones" onto gloves. Sew two pieces of black felt together as a hood to slip over head. Cut out eye holes and add white tape in skull shape.

SKELETON

PRINCE   PRINCESS

ROBOT

Make a crown by covering cardboard with aluminum foil. Cover a cardboard sword with foil. Wear boots. Wear a belt buckled over a long shirt. Make a princess hat with a cardboard cone and scarf coming out of the top. Princess wears a long dress.

Cover boxes with aluminum foil.

HALLOWEEN GAMES

These games present a twist on the traditional, but are a challenge not only for children but for the grown-ups, too!

Apple Fishing

There is no need to dunk and get a face full of water for this game! Prepare about a dozen small apples by pushing a partially opened paper clip into the top of an apple so that the part sticking out is hooklike. Now, tie a pegboard hook to one end of a string and tie the other end to a wooden dowel or tree branch to form a fishing pole. Try to hook a bobbing apple in a tub of water.

Monster Toss

Make a set of bean bags. (Fill bags with birdseed as it is cheaper than dried beans.) Give each child a plain paper plate and let her color in a monster face. Tape a piece of yarn to the top of the plate and tape or tie the other end of yarn to a door sill so the monster plates can swing freely. Participants form two lines and each player gets to toss a bean bag at a "monster." A hit is one point. The team with the most points wins.

Pin the Nose on the Jack-o'-Lantern

Cut out a large pumpkin shape from one or two sheets of orange construction paper. Draw the eyes and mouth in the correct position with a black marker. While blindfolded, parents and children try to pin or tape a black construction paper nose where it should go on the Jack-o'-Lantern.

Monster Practice

Have a gurning contest. Gurning is trying to make the ugliest face possible. Allow participants to look into mirrors and take instant photos of all the ugly faces. Vote on the best "monster mug."

Popcorn Balls

As a special treat, have everyone help prepare the recipe on page 77.

POPCORN BALLS

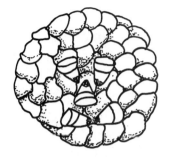  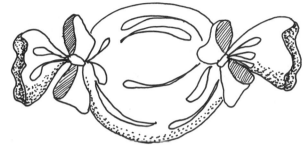

YOU'LL NEED:

8 cups popped popcorn

1 c. molasses
1 c. corn syrup
1 tblsp. vinegar

butter
bowl
saucepan
candy thermometer

WHAT TO DO:

1. Remove any unpopped kernels and place 8 cups popcorn in a bowl.

2. Place molasses, corn syrup and vinegar in a saucepan. Adult brings mixture to a boil, stirring constantly.

3. Remove from heat when temperature of mixture reaches 270°F on thermometer. (soft-crack stage)

4. Adult carefully pours syrup into bowl full of popcorn. Mix well. Cool slightly.

5. Children butter hands. Pick up cooled popcorn and shape into balls. Wrap, if desired.

HALLOWEEN SAFETY TIPS

Halloween can be a fun night for everyone. Adults or older children should always accompany young children and be aware of all the possible dangers. Here are some suggestions to keep the spooky celebration safe.

■ Plan for children to wear masks that are half-faced on the lower part of the face or make-up instead of full-faced masks in order to see traffic clearly. Use reflective tape, strips, patches, or paint (available in bike, auto supply, and sporting goods stores) for extra visibility.

■ Buy only nonflammable costumes and wigs. Consider using hair spray for a similar effect.

■ Avoid costume accessories that could cause accidents—falls, cuts, or bruises. Say NO to shoes that don't fit or are too high-heeled for walking, roller skates, sharp or pointed toy weapons, loose dresses that are too long.

■ Provide Trick-or-Treat bags that are small so they don't cause accidental falls or knocks.

■ Carry a flashlight or battery-powered lantern.

■ Use flashlights instead of candles to light pumpkins.

■ When traveling, stay in your own neighborhood, and, if possible, in well-lit areas.

■ Travel in a small group—up one side of the street and down the other. Criss-crossing a street is dangerous.

■ Stay away from strange dogs who might get frightened by the costumes.

■ Pass by houses that are not lit up. This usually means that the owners are not prepared for young visitors.

■ Walk only on sidewalks when possible. In the road, walk on the LEFT side of the street, FACING traffic. Be sure to review traffic rules: cross only at lights at the crosswalks; look both ways before crossing; do not walk between parked cars to get into the road.

■ Unfortunately, some treats have become dangerous in the past few years, so children should be allowed to eat ONLY treats that are paperwrapped. THROW OUT all other unpackaged items or those with torn wrappings. If you discover anything wrong with something brought home, notify the police so that they can warn others.

■ Set a specific time for the children to come home.

"Halloween should be fun—and safe—for everyone."

AN INVITATION

A CONCERT

♪ LISTEN TO THE MUSIC

♪ SEE MUSICAL INSTRUMENTS

♪ TALK TO THE MUSICIANS

♪ SING OR HUM ALONG WITH FRIENDS

Come to a concert on .... at ....

A CONCERT

"Music is a love parents and children can share."

Concerts can broaden children's musical horizons by bringing them closer to the melodies, musicians, and instruments. Inviting parents to share this experience makes it a really special event.

You can arrange your own concert with a little help from interested parents. To find musicians, check with the music departments of local high schools, music schools, parents themselves, and friends. Very often, talented students are willing to perform for the experience and practice. Local bands and music teachers might be willing to perform without charge in exchange for free publicity. If a fee must be paid, you could charge admission to cover your expenses.

To help maintain children's interest and enthusiasm for music, consider the following when planning your concert.

■ Plan a short and varied program. Young children cannot sit still too long. A half hour program plus an intermission would be within a pre-schooler's attention span. At the end of the concert, if the children want more, encores can fill the need for additional entertainment.

■ Choose a variety of spirited music—classical, modern, folk, and jazz. Have a balanced program of contrasting selections. Be sure to include some that the children are already familiar with and some that encourage audience participation. Work the program out with the musicians.

"Spark children's interest in music with a concert."

■ Make sure that the children can sit near the musicians. In a large area, arrange the children's chairs in a wide semi-circle directly in front of the musicians with the parents' chairs behind.

■ Use an intermission to let the children get up, stretch, walk off their pent-up energy, and talk to their friends. Let them meet and talk to the performing artists. Before the concert, speak with the performers about letting the children observe the instruments up close. If possible, let children touch them and try them out. Some of the parents may even want a turn. How many of us have actually touched a harp or pulled out an accordian? Don't hurry a child's contact with the instrument or try to influence her selection. If the group is small, there will be enough time during intermission and after the performance for everyone to have a turn. Children should be supervised, but permitted to explore on their own, while you watch that the instruments are safe.

By providing concerts for young children and their parents, you can help families share an appreciation for music.

YOU ARE INVITED TO...

Enjoy an UPSIDE DOWN NIGHT with your children. They show you what school is like as you become students for an evening!

UPSIDE DOWN NIGHT

KIDS LOVE THE TWIST!

LISTEN TO EACH OTHER

☆ SING SONGS

☆ SHARE EXPERIENCES

WORK AND PLAY TOGETHER ☆

MEET FRIENDS ☆

☆ KIDS CAN TEACH

☆ SHARE A SNACK

DATE:

TIME:

WHERE:

JUST FOR ONE NIGHT: "BE A KID AGAIN"

UPSIDE DOWN NIGHT

"For one crazy, fun night, the children act like adults and vice versa."

Children always delight in having their parents come to school. This special event gives parents the chance not only to come to school but to participate with their children in activities that their children do each school day. And, the funny twist is that the children can act as adults and the parents can be the children!

The classroom is set up as it would be on a regular day with sand areas, blocks, and art materials out. The children have, of course, been well prepared for the activities of the evening. You can post a number at each activity to indicate how many "kids" can participate at one time.

Upside Down Night goes into action with the kids "teaching" the parents how to use the paints and clays, how to construct with blocks, and how to do puzzles. This is the time for a child and her parents to really play together in the child's world. She has her parents' undivided attention for a short time and everyone gets to see how the others feel. Children can share their favorite activities and show off their friends.

Include some of the following ideas, along with your own, for Upside Down Night:

■ Children show their parents how to put coats into their cubbies

■ You and the children can make name tags in advance for the parents so they can hang them up for you to take attendance. These name tags can be worn by the parents for the evening.

■ You might want to have the children teach the parents a song by rote

■ Children can introduce their parents at circletime (and parents can introduce their children, also)

■ Children can serve foods they've prepared to the parents at snacktime

■ Children can assist you by announcing transition times, cleanup, and snack

■ Children can help parents do a craft, such as scrap puppet-making or fingerprint pictures and both parents and children can present them as a grand finale for the evening

For this one crazy night, the children are the adults, and the grownups are the learners and the novices.

AN INVITATION

GAMES PARTY

- OBSTACLE COURSE
- BEAN BAG GAMES
- RACKET BALLOON
- FRISBEE TOSS
- TUNNEL BALL
- BALLOON RACE

Games for parents and children to play together.

Refreshments = Fun = Get Acquainted

Time: Date:

Come Play With Us!

GAME PARTY

"Schedule your game party when you can be outdoors."

Games, both quiet and active, that are fun and non-competitive, are an excellent way for parents and children to interact and to spend time together.

Schedule a game party in the spring or fall when you can be out-of-doors. The fresh air adds a special touch to the activities. This could be done at any convenient time of the day (late afternoon or early evening) and on any day of the week or weekend.

PREPARATION

■ Talk to the children about having a family game party. Ask them the following questions:

- "What are your favorite games? in school? at home?"
- "What kinds of games do you play with your family?"
- "What kinds of games have you seen your parents play?"
- "Which ones would you like to play at our game party?"

■ Teach the children a new game and practice it so that they can teach it to their parents at the party. See pages 86, 87, and 88 for some suggestions. For more game suggestions, read *The Complete Sport and Games Book—Challenge without Competition* by Terry Orlick (Pantheon).

■ Copy the Game Party invitation on page 83 or make up your own. Let the children decorate them and take them home.

"Keep the party short."

■ Keep the party short, one or one and one-half hours duration. Busy children (and parents) get tired easily and you want everyone to leave feeling good. Don't try to schedule too many activities. If everyone wants more games, plan a similar event later in the year.

■ Select games and activities that your children love and always have fun playing, such as Red Light, Green Light and Simon Says. Their excitement will be contagious.

■ Choose games that are easy to play, requiring a minimum of skill so that everyone feels successful and leaves with a sense of accomplishment. You'd be surprised at how many parents are reluctant to try something new in front of their children especially if there's the slightest chance that they can't do it.

"Select games parents and children can play together."

■ Find games that everyone can participate in. This makes for a stronger feeling of cooperation and togetherness and encourages socializing. Try "The Smaug's Jewels," "Flying Dutchman" and "The Blob" games from *The New Games Book* by Andrew Fleugelman (Doubleday and Co.).

■ Select games that a parent and child also can play together by themselves. Children sometimes require their parents' undivided attention at these occasions.

"Demonstrate when giving directions."

HELPFUL HINTS

■ The best directions to give are demonstrations. You can let the children help with these. (They'll feel so important.) Try to keep verbal instructions to a minimum.

■ You might want to begin the party with a simple group stretching song such as Lobby Loo. This relaxes everyone and gets the group's energy flowing.

■ At the end of the evening, serve a snack and something to drink.

GAMES

YOU'LL NEED:

gallon milk jugs

bean bags
(make your own and fill with birdseed)

bicycle tire

bell with clapper

BEAN BAG GAMES

WHAT TO DO:

BEAN BAG SCOOP

GALLON MILK JUG
CUT
SCOOP

Parent and child are partners. Each has a scoop and one bean bag. Parents and children line up facing each other in two parallel lines. After each toss and catch, both take one step backwards, _each_ _time_! Parent and child are out of the game when bean bag is dropped.

TARGET TIRE

Two groups of parents and children line up and attempt to toss a bean bag into a bicycle tire rolled in front of them by another parent. Each person gets one try. Count the number of times the bean bag goes through the tire to determine the winning team.

FOOT TOSS

Two teams, with an equal number of plays, sit in two circles on chairs. Each circle has one bean bag. The players must pass the bean bag around the circle once - using only feet. No hands are allowed. The circle who gets the bean bag around to everyone first, wins.

RING THE BELL

Parents and children form two teams and line up a couple of yards away from a bell suspended from a tree or the ceiling. Each person, on both teams, tries to ring the bell with the bean bag.

MORE GAMES

YOU'LL NEED:

6'-8' piece of 2'x4' lumber

 car tires

tether balls  Tether ball is made with toe end of nylon stocking stuffed with more stockings and tied with an elastic band or string.

 furniture  rope

OBSTACLE COURSE

WHAT TO DO:

1 BALANCE BEAM (2'x4')

2 TIRES

3 FURNITURE

4 SWINGING TETHER BALLS

An obstacle course need not be competitive to be fun. Children and parents alike can test their skills and feel a sense of accomplishment by having just gone through the course. Set up the obstacle course will all or some of the above.

AND MORE GAMES

YOU'LL NEED:

 balloons

frisbee

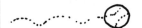 ball   masking tape

large box

wire hangers

nylon stockings

twist ties

BALLOONS, BALLS, RACKETS and FRISBEES

BALLOON RACE

Form two teams. A parent and child are partners, and they have one balloon. The object of this race is for the parent-child partners to take the balloon to a finish line - but without using their hands! They can use their bodies to hold the balloon as they walk fast to the finish line. One couple goes at a time, in a relay manner. First team with all players over finish line, wins!

RACKET BALLOON

Use balloons and these special rackets to practice hitting. Balloons move slowly as do the rackets, making this a wonderful activity for young children.

1. PULL A WIRE COAT HANGER OPEN

2. BEND HOOK INTO A CLOSED OVAL.

3. STRETCH A NYLON STOCKING OVER HANGER AND SECURE WITH A PLASTIC BAG TWIST TIE.

4. TAPE WIRE HOOK OVAL WITH SEVERAL LAYERS OF TAPE.

TUNNEL BALL RACE

Parents and their children line up in two teams. All face forward and spread feet apart. First person rolls ball through own legs to next person. Ball is continually pushed and rolled through everyone's legs. Last person picks up the ball, runs to the front of the line and starts the ball rolling again through legs. When the first person gets to the front again, the game stops.

FRISBEE TOSS

Use frisbees (or plastic lids from coffee cans or frozen food containers). Throw the frisbee through "window" you've cut out on a large box. You can also cut holes in a sheet and hang sheet on clothes line. Label number of points for each hole.

YOU ARE INVITED TO

AN

INFORMAL

PERFORMANCE

INFORMAL PERFORMANCES

Formal performances where children act or perform with a predetermined script or routine have little place in most preschools and kindergartens. There are occasions however when parents come to school and would like to see a demonstration of what their children have been doing. A musical performance that is based on the children's everyday music program is one answer. Others might include spontaneous play in a magical setting or creative dramatics to the reading of a favorite fairy tale or poem.

CLASS CONCERT

If your regular program contains songs, song games, movement, and rhythm activities, you can turn it into a show for parents. Have children sing a few familiar songs. Do some of the usual movement games and rhythm activities that the children know very well and can do almost instinctively without help. Remember to keep the musical program as casual as it would be during a regular classtime. If the children usually sit in a circle on the floor, or around the piano on chairs, by all means keep the same, familiar format. You want the children to feel comfortable. Try to take only volunteers to lead the group or play an instrument because draftees might freeze up in front of an audience.

The following are a few suggested activities that we have found make a varied, colorful, and successful musical evening.

"If You're Happy"

This is a great starter with the clapping and feet stomping. The adult leader may pretend to fall asleep on the last, "if you're sleepy and you know it, rub your eyes, if you're sleepy and you know it, then your face is going to show it." Of course, the children will shout to wake up the leader and finish the song.

"Down by the Station"

This activity gets children lined up like a train. The leading child is the engine and the rest are cars. The children shuffle their feet as they follow the leader around chairs, tables, and in and out of doorways. Of course, the children sing and make believe they are pulling on a cord as they shout "toot, toot."

"Frozen Skaters' Waltz"

Use a recording or piano piece and play the music as the children pretend to "skate" on the floor. Stop the music every once in a while and let the children freeze in an unusual position.

"Honky Tonk Pompoms"

You will need a recording of honky tonk piano music. Children swing soft pompoms on a length of yarn in time with the music. See how fast they can twirl them. Children love both the music and activity.

"Classical Balloons"

Play slow, classical music, such as Strauss waltzes, while children try to keep balloons floating in the air. They must move very slowly, almost in slow motion. Then, have children keeping in the same slow motion, gently toss the balloons to each other.

"Belly Dance Scarves"

Use a recording of belly dance music or Greek bouzuki music and have children dance around with scarves. Children can walk like camels, moving sideways and bending back, while kneeling. This music is great for bending and stretching and the scarves add the balance.

NURSERY RHYMES

Nursery rhymes are a wonderful source of lyrical rhyme often with simple melodies, plenty of action, and lots of variety. They lend themselves to being acted out with just a few props. Here are some suggestions to enhance children's love of these first memorized rhymes that would also be lovely to share.

■ *Humpty Dumpty* "Humpty" sits on a pile of blocks to represent a wall. The king's men ride stick horses all around. (See page 92 for the nursery rhyme prop you can make.)

■ *Yankee Doodle* Have children march around riding stick horses and wearing paper hats that they've helped to make.

■ *Banbury Cross* Have children trot on their stick horses and wear jingle bell rings and jingle bell anklets.

■ *Mary, Mary, Quite Contrary* Have "Mary" use a watering can to sprinkle her flowers. The flowers could be children, covered with colorful scarves. The pop up, as they are watered.

End your musical performance evening with a sing-along. Have parents join the children for a few familiar songs such as "This Land Is Your Land" and "I'm a Little Teapot." Serve something to "wet your whistle" and finish up the evening.

STICK HORSES

YOU'LL NEED:

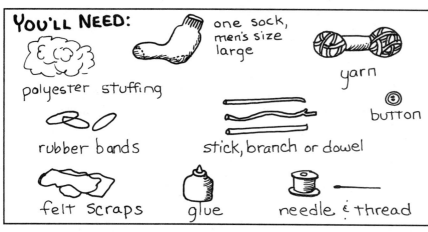

- polyester stuffing
- one sock, men's size large
- yarn
- button
- rubber bands
- stick, branch or dowel
- felt scraps
- glue
- needle & thread

WHAT TO DO:

 1. Child stuffs sock with polyester stuffing.

 2. Place stick or dowel inside sock between stuffing. Stick should extend almost to heel.

 3. Secure stick with rubber bands about 4" from edge of sock.

 4. Child glues or uses needle and thread to add felt ears, eyes, tongue. Adult sews button on for nose.

 5. Adult or child uses needle and thread to sew on yarn hair in loops.

MUSICAL POM POMS

 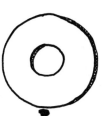   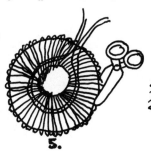 

1.   2.   3.   4.   5.

KNOT →

YOU'LL NEED:

 a piece corrugated cardboard

 yarn

 scissors

 thread and needle

WHAT TO DO:

1. Adult makes these: Cut a circle from cardboard. It should be about 6"-8" round. Cut a 1½"-2" circle out of center. (2 above)

2. Make a small ball of yarn and wind it loosely around cardboard, going into center and over edges. (3 above)

3. Thread needle with yarn. Insert needle under wound up yarn around center circle. (4 above)

4. Pull needle and yarn out of circle, leaving length of yarn still under all wound yarn. Gather two ends tightly.

5. Hold two ends firmly as someone else cuts yarn around outer edge. Pull the two ends very tightly and knot. Pull pom pom away from cardboard.

6. Tie a long piece of yarn to the knot end securely. Child holds pompom and swings it.

93

FAIRY TALES

Let the children decide who they would like to be and let them take turns acting out the different parts. Be prepared to tell and retell each story many times because children love to keep repeating it. Let the children decide which favorite fairy tale or story they'd like to share with their families.

The following fairy tales make wonderful stories to dramatize. It's best not to get very dressed up or become too literal. You may want to start by telling the tale as children enact one scene. Expand gradually to the whole tale. When the tale is very familiar, let children add some of their own dialogue if they want to. The most important part of dramatizing fairy tales is to have fun with them. Let the children enjoy themselves, and don't be concerned about being correct.

■ *Little Red Riding Hood* Tell the story and provide colorful scarves as props: a red one for Little Red Riding Hood, a scarf for grandma's babushka, and a dark one over the "wolf." Use scarves also to suggest grandma's bed.

■ *The Three Little Pigs* Collect a few "bricks" (blocks), twigs, and straw. Tell the story, and have each pig "build" his house out of one of the materials. Have the wolf come by and say: "Little pig, little pig, let me in." Then, the wolf huffs and puffs and blows the house down.

■ *Goldilocks and the Three Bears* Give children the opportunity to bring in their stuffed animals and dolls to tell this story. Use child-sized furniture and dishes. An opened-out tent can be the house.

STARTERS

Map use of some of these "what ifs" and "pretends" to encourage creative work in your "woods" scene described on the following page.
■ "What if you were an animal that lived in these woods? What kind would you be? Show me."
■ "What if you were a fish in the river? How would you swim?"
■ "What if you had to get across the river? How would you do it?"
■ "What if you could fly? Where would you go?"
■ "What if you were a tree? How would you look?"
■ "What if you were rain? What kind of a storm would you be?"

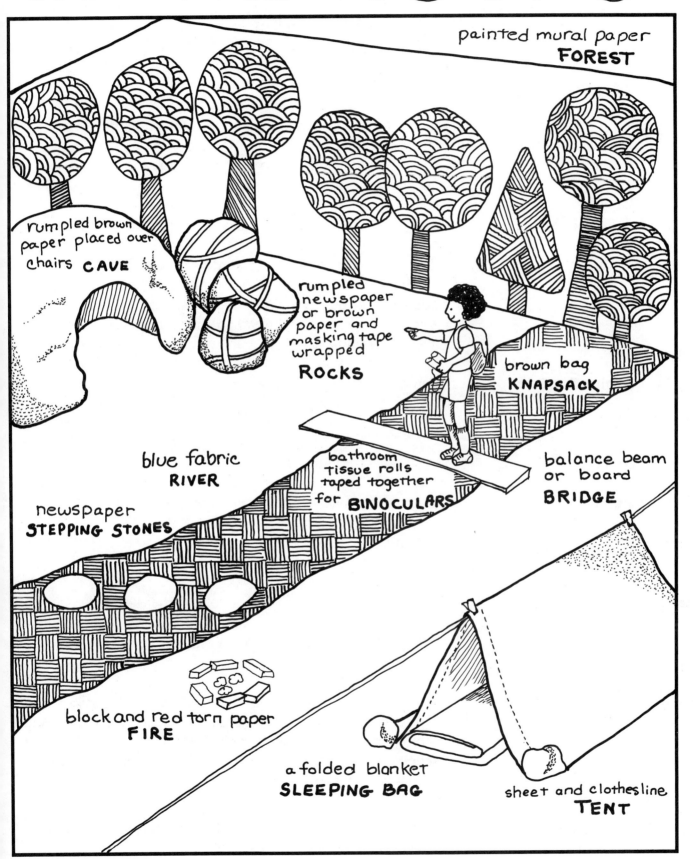

FUN FUNDRAISERS

Everyone needs money these days, especially daycare centers and nursery schools. So when your fundraising team of parents and teachers gets together next time, consider one of these ideas.

An Auction

Parents, friends of the school, and local merchants can donate merchandise and/or services to the school to be auctioned off on a specific night. This can be a very big job but it does bring in a lot of money.

Family Dessert Night

Members of the board of directors or Parent/Teacher's Association can bake desserts. The rest of the school pays a small fee to attend the family dessert night to eat the desserts, socialize, and be entertained. The admission fees might be $2.00 per adult and $1.00 per child or a maximum of $5.00 per family. For entertainment, you might want to hire a puppeteer, clown, or musician for a sing-along.

Spring Cleaning Tag Sale

Clean out your closets, basements, and attics and donate your discards to the school's tag sale. It's amazing how one person's junk is another person's treasure.

Musical Concert

See pages 79-80 for details.

T-shirt Sale

Design, print, and sell school/class t-shirts and sweats.

Recipe Book

Create a class recipe book and sell the completed book at all school functions. (See page 72 for directions.)

Raffle

If you can get a substantial piece of merchandise or service donated at a reasonable price, raffle it off. Contact a local print shop for raffle ticket printing. Watch out that your printing costs don't wipe out your profits.

Book Sale

Contact book companies that publish the type of books you wish to sell—children's books, parenting books, childrearing and psychology books, and good workbook/activity books for pre-schoolers. The book companies will provide you with the books at a wholesale price. Then, you can resell them at the retail price.

Craft/Art Show and Sale

Contact local craftspeople and artists to sell their products and artwork. This is an especially good kind of fundraiser to have before the holidays. You also can hold a gift-making workshop for adults at your school to make such things as bookmarks, mirrors, and decorated clothing that can also be sold at the show. A small announcement in the local papers which says you are seeking handcrafted products often can produce great finds.

Ski and Skate Sale

Parents, friends, and others bring in their old or outgrown sports equipment and clothing to be sold on consignment.

Orange and Grapefruit Sale

Contact the Ruby Red Produce Company for information on how to order their produce for your group to sell.

Matinee Movie

Rent a wonderful classic movie to be shown on a wintry afternoon. (This is great to do during the holidays since many parents are looking for something for their children to do.) Sell popcorn. You could have an activity after the movie—balloon games after the movie ''The Red Balloon.''

Adults Only Dance Party

You provide the disc jockey to keep the music playing all night and ask the parents, friends, and the public to pay admission. Volunteers can provide drinks and nibbles. (The best place to begin finding a DJ is at your local rock-and-roll radio station.)

Festival Table Dinner

The dinner tables are decorated in most unusual, elaborate, wild ways according to the theme of the evening. A core group of people (10-20) each take charge of one table to decorate and then sell tickets to their friends. Each table then becomes a lavish private dinner party in the big room. One school chose a fairy tale theme and one participant did her table à la Little Red Riding Hood complete with a decorated antique basket filled with food, flowers, and other goodies as the centerpiece on a red-checkered tablecloth.

Multicultural Potluck Supper

Each family is assigned a country and asked to prepare ethnic dishes. Include folk singers to entertain by singing popular songs from all the different countries.

Carnival

Set up lots of different fun activity booths and sell tickets to the children for $.50 each. (Some booths might cost two tickets.) Keep the prizes simple and inexpensive. Here are some activities that work well.

■ Toss ping pong balls into bowls or jars. Winners get a certificate for a goldfish at a local pet shop.

■ Make buttons. You can purchase the machine and let the children design their own buttons that you then put together for them.

■ Children love to have their faces made up as clowns or to be able to choose a specific design like rainbows or hearts.

■ Guess how many jelly beans or peanuts are in the jar.

■ Break water balloons.

For more ideas, brainstorm with parents and check with other places which have run a carnival to find out which booths were the most popular. Remember to involve the children in the decorations and planning.

To advertise these events, send home a flier with each child and mail fliers to your alumni list. Have someone write up a human interest story about the event for your local newspaper. Try to get photos of the children working on the fundraiser printed along with the story. For the really big events—craft show, auction, carnival, disco—that might involve the whole town, have posters printed and place them in store windows.

TAKING SCHOOL HOME

TAKE HOME LEARNING

Just as you want parents to share their children's experience at school, it is also important for the learning that begins at school to continue after the child goes home. Often, parents don't realize that there's a lot of learning that takes place in the home. You can help them stimulate and encourage learning at home with reminders and suggestions of educational activities that they can do together with their children.

You can prepare take-home parent/child activity sheets. These sheets of activities (that do not have to be related to your class theme) can help bring the child's world at school closer to home. These sheets can include:

■ Words to songs that children are singing at school. The child can teach the melodies to her parents.

■ Pencil/paper games. Believe it or not, children love the idea of "homework," especially if they have older siblings who really bring home assignments. These games bring parents and children together for fun and learning. Parents can create their own from your model. Some suggestions might be a simple 1-10 dot-to-dot drawing; a maze; a set of parallel lines that the child must trace a line between without touching the sides; a fill-in-the-missing-parts of the letters or a one-to-one correspondence drawing. (Present a drawing of six children with fishing poles and six fish. Children must draw fishlines from each pole to one fish.)

■ A recommendation for a small trip (during the week). It can be a shopping trip to the local bakery. Suggest that parent and child look at bread shapes and count rolls. It might be as simple as a walk around the block to collect leaves from all the various trees. Some suggestions you can make for bigger weekend holiday trips and visits can be found on pages 106-107.

■ A wonderful recipe that's been a great success with the children at school for the parent and child to try together at home

Whatever you choose for the "Take-Home" sheet, make sure that it is easy to do and fun for both parents and children.

The first two "Dear Parent" letters that follow give parents ideas for helping their child bridge the gap between home and school. The third one is a sample of how a theme in the classroom can be expanded at home. Again, as long as the lines of communcation between parents and teachers stay open and active, everyone will benefit.

"Stimulate learning at home with activity sheets."

"What Did You Do Today ?"

Dear Parents:

Making that bridge into your child's school life can often be hard to do. There are many ways of getting into and being a part of a child's private world without prying. Consider these suggestions for good parent/child contact.

ASK specific questions, not general ones like "What did you do today?" She probably did too much during the day to remember everything and even to start to give you an answer. Be more specific like: "It was such a beautiful day today. Did you play outside at all? What did you play on?"

USE your child's artwork and other papers that are brought home as a stimulation for conversation. "Tell me about this picture."

LISTEN to any new words your child says or observations she makes and pick up on them to get into a conversation — "I hate the bus ride home." "What is it about the bus ride that you don't like. Tell me about it." "It's too long." "Are any of your friends on the bus with you?" "Yes, Jessica." "Do you sit with her? What did you talk about?"

TALK to your child's friends when they come to play. Take a few minutes to be with them. Often, a friend will be more willing to share information than your own child, but when a friend does, your child will join in.

ENQUIRE about lunchtime when you're emptying her lunchbox. Keep the questions open-ended so that you might get more meaty conversation than just about the food — "How was lunch today?"

ENCOURAGE your child to bring home a book from the school library that you can read together. Talk about the other books and when and if the teacher reads books to the class — "Who picks them out?" "Which is your favorite?"

GO OVER class newsletters together that are brought home, instead of just perusing it yourself and then throwing it away.

It may seem like pulling teeth sometimes, but it's worth the effort to bridge the gap between school and home.

Truly yours,

Your child's teacher

CHILDREN'S ARTWORK

Dear Parents:

During the year your child will be bringing home lots of art work that he has done in class. They are absolute treasures not only for you to look at and enjoy, but also for your child who is very proud of his work. But these paintings, sculptures, collages, and other works of art are something else; they are connections to your child's world at school and to his thoughts and feelings.

SHOW AN INTEREST IN EVERYTHING YOUR CHILD BRINGS HOME. Admire the artwork and talk about it. It is something your child has worked on and, as his creation, it is a part of him. "It looks like you worked very hard on this picture. I like the way you pasted all of these feathers on. Tell me about it." He may or may not wish to talk about it; whatever he decides is okay.

DISPLAY THE ARTWORK. Children are very proud of their creations and enjoy when they are appreciated. Hang them up in a special place where your child and everyone else can see them. Many people hang flat art on the refrigerator with a magnet. Change the pictures each time your child makes a new one. It's more important that the picture is displayed than the amount of time it's up.

FILE IT. Keep a folder with your child's name on it to store all the artwork already displayed. Be sure to put the date on the back. Your child might really enjoy looking at his creations when he is older.

USE IT AS A GIFT. You can use your child's artwork to make gifts for relatives and friends.

Make a framed picture by mounting your child's picture on a slightly larger sheet of colored paper with glue or making a frame with colored masking tape.

To make a calendar, paste 12 pieces of artwork of similar size on 12 calendar pages and staple them together.

COLLAGED "GADGET" BOX

PENCIL HOLDER

NOTE PAPER

CAROL

Make wastepaper baskets with an empty ice cream container (large) from a local ice cream store. Clean it. Glue a large piece of artwork around the container.

You can cover a placemat-sized piece of artwork with clear contact paper. Or, buy the clear vinyl that comes in a roll. Cut it to the size of the table. Put it on the table and slip your child's artwork under it. Because it doesn't stick, you can keep changing the artwork.

To make a greeting card, paste a small picture of the child's choice onto a white sheet of paper that has been folded in half.

You can make note paper by pasting a small picture or part of a picture (Before you cut it, ask your child's permission.) on the top of a blank sheet of white paper, and send a note.

Mount pictures on several sheets of paper of the same size. Bind them with rings and make a book. Ask your child to tell you about each picture and at the bottom of the page, write exactly what he says. If he says nothing, leave the page wordless. He will enjoy "reading" it to you.

Use a very colorful drawing to wrap a flat present. Do not use a painted picture because the paint might crack.

Fold a large picture done on folder type paper (or paper of heavier quality) in half and use it to store letters, recipes or receipts.

These are just a few suggestions that have worked well for families that have been part of our class. Whatever you do with your child's artwork, CHERISH IT!

Sincerely yours,

Your child's teacher

RECIPES: CAKES

FILE FOLDERS

BOOKMARKS

WRAPPING PAPER

Night Letter

Dear Parents:

We have been discussing the stars, the sun, the planets, the moon, and comets in class recently. We would like you, if possible, to show your child the nighttime skies. Here are some suggestions to make this a fun, learning experience.

When you take a nighttime walk:

● talk about the absence of lights.

● listen to the nighttime sounds of animals, birds, insects, and people.

● observe the nighttime creatures that might come out — the bats, owls, raccoons, possums, deer, skunks, porcupines, and rats.

● locate the moon, some of the stars, and even a planet or two. (Planets are usually found slightly above the horizon in very early evening or just before sunrise.)

● sit down and watch for falling stars. These are really meteors that have entered our atmosphere.

● watch how the clouds sometimes cover the moon and the stars.

● point out the different position the moon is in after a short time.

● pick out one familiar constellation and tell your child that it is a group of stars that has a specific name. (The Big and Little Dipper are always handy.)

● look at the stars and moon through a paper towel roll (It is not a telescope or binoculars, yet you will be surprised how much more you can see without the surrounding light.)

● have the child notice how much more she can see after her eyes have adjusted to the darkness — look for details on each others' faces. Try to read a newspaper in the dark. Try to read the paper in the moonlight.

● play shadow tag in the moonlight. Trace your child's shadow on a piece of paper, using moonlight only.

● bring a bunch of colored socks outside into the moonlight. See if you can sort them by color in that dim light. Bring them inside for a good laugh. In such pale light, we see things only as blacks, and grays with very little or no coloring.

● play a hearing game called "creep on by."

Give your child a flashlight and sit outside on the ground. Tell her to close her eyes. Play this game with a few people. Have all the other players start in front of the child. Everyone tries to creep by the child without her hearing anyone. If she hears anyone, she lights the flashlight and points it in the direction of the sound. If the light touches the creeper, he must go back and start all over again. The rest can continue to creep past the child. Take turns and let the child be a creeper. (This game comes from the Smithsonian Family Learning Project Science Calendar for 1986.)

Just enjoy this time outside at night with your child. Listen to what she has to say. Kids are just wonderful day or night!

Sincerely,

Your child's teacher

WEEKEND FUN

Here are suggestions for interesting and fun day trips or weekends for young children. Find something _you_ like to do, and you and your child will have a great time.

IN THE COUNTRY...

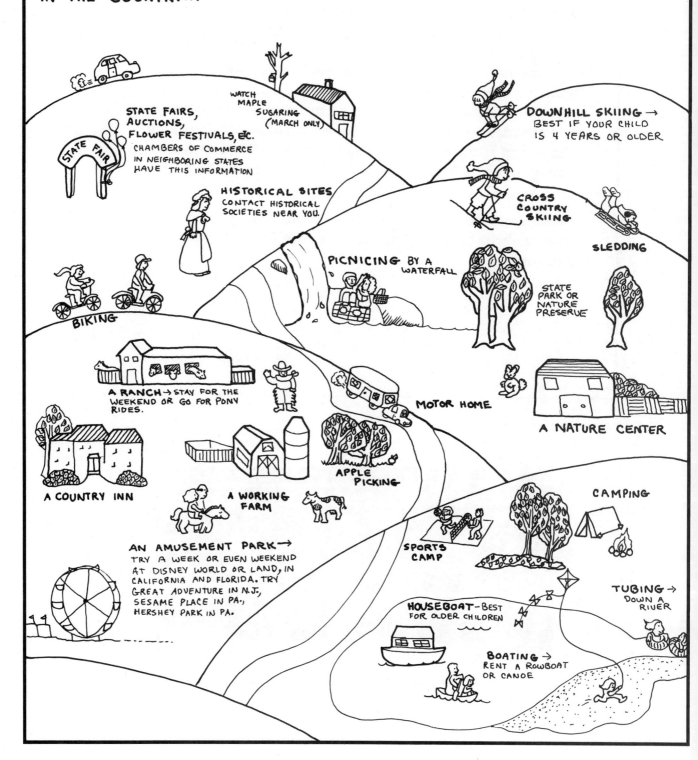

STATE FAIRS, AUCTIONS, FLOWER FESTIVALS, ETC. CHAMBERS OF COMMERCE IN NEIGHBORING STATES HAVE THIS INFORMATION

WATCH MAPLE SUGARING (MARCH ONLY)

DOWNHILL SKIING → BEST IF YOUR CHILD IS 4 YEARS OR OLDER

HISTORICAL SITES CONTACT HISTORICAL SOCIETIES NEAR YOU.

CROSS COUNTRY SKIING

SLEDDING

PICNICING BY A WATERFALL

STATE PARK OR NATURE PRESERVE

BIKING

A RANCH → STAY FOR THE WEEKEND OR GO FOR PONY RIDES.

MOTOR HOME

A NATURE CENTER

A COUNTRY INN

A WORKING FARM

APPLE PICKING

CAMPING

AN AMUSEMENT PARK → TRY A WEEK OR EVEN WEEKEND AT DISNEY WORLD OR LAND, IN CALIFORNIA AND FLORIDA. TRY GREAT ADVENTURE IN N.J., SESAME PLACE IN PA., HERSHEY PARK IN PA.

SPORTS CAMP

TUBING → DOWN A RIVER

HOUSEBOAT - BEST FOR OLDER CHILDREN

BOATING → RENT A ROWBOAT OR CANOE

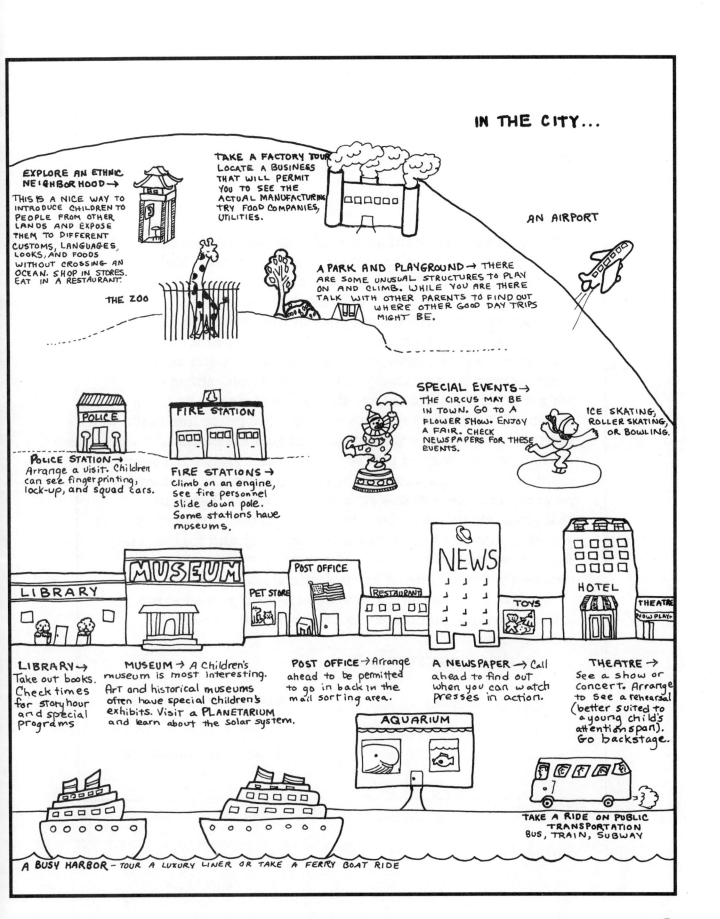

IN THE CITY...

EXPLORE AN ETHNIC NEIGHBORHOOD →
THIS IS A NICE WAY TO INTRODUCE CHILDREN TO PEOPLE FROM OTHER LANDS AND EXPOSE THEM TO DIFFERENT CUSTOMS, LANGUAGES, LOOKS, AND FOODS WITHOUT CROSSING AN OCEAN. SHOP IN STORES. EAT IN A RESTAURANT.

THE ZOO

TAKE A FACTORY TOUR
LOCATE A BUSINESS THAT WILL PERMIT YOU TO SEE THE ACTUAL MANUFACTURING. TRY FOOD COMPANIES, UTILITIES.

AN AIRPORT

A PARK AND PLAYGROUND → THERE ARE SOME UNUSUAL STRUCTURES TO PLAY ON AND CLIMB. WHILE YOU ARE THERE TALK WITH OTHER PARENTS TO FIND OUT WHERE OTHER GOOD DAY TRIPS MIGHT BE.

POLICE

FIRE STATION

POLICE STATION →
Arrange a visit. Children can see finger printing, lock-up, and squad cars.

FIRE STATIONS →
Climb on an engine, see fire personnel slide down pole. Some stations have museums.

SPECIAL EVENTS →
THE CIRCUS MAY BE IN TOWN. GO TO A FLOWER SHOW. ENJOY A FAIR. CHECK NEWSPAPERS FOR THESE EVENTS.

ICE SKATING, ROLLER SKATING, OR BOWLING.

LIBRARY

MUSEUM

POST OFFICE

PET STORE

RESTAURANT

NEWS

TOYS

HOTEL

THEATRE
NOW PLAYING

LIBRARY →
Take out books. Check times for story hour and special programs

MUSEUM → A Children's museum is most interesting. Art and historical museums often have special children's exhibits. Visit a PLANETARIUM and learn about the solar system.

POST OFFICE → Arrange ahead to be permitted to go in back in the mail sorting area.

A NEWSPAPER → Call ahead to find out when you can watch presses in action.

THEATRE →
See a show or concert. Arrange to see a rehearsal (better suited to a young child's attention span). Go backstage.

AQUARIUM

TAKE A RIDE ON PUBLIC TRANSPORTATION BUS, TRAIN, SUBWAY

A BUSY HARBOR - TOUR A LUXURY LINER OR TAKE A FERRY BOAT RIDE

Dear Parents, Good-Bye

Dear Parents:

We've had a wonderful year together. And I'd like to thank you for all your cooperation and participation that has helped to make this year so successful.

I'm sure that your child, who has been so special to all of us, greatly benefited from your being here with us and that he has gotten to know you a little better as a result.

I also hope that you've enjoyed your visits with us as much as we have and that you've learned something about your child and all the things that we're trying to do here in school. I certainly hope that this experience has made you feel welcome any time in your child's classroom.

Enclosed is a map of places that you can visit with your child. We've visited some of them with our class. You might want to visit some of the others on your own. Let your child look at the map with you to see what interests him.

I hope that you have a wonderful holiday and think of us when your child sings some of her favorite school songs or when you cook one of our favorite school dishes.

And please remember, I'm always here if you need me for information, advice, or to help with any of your parenting concerns.

Thanks again for your help.

Sincerely,

Your Child's Teacher

From the authors of
CRAYONS
CRAFTS
AND
CONCEPTS

CONCEPT COOKERY

by
Kathy Faggella

Through cooking experiences in the preschool classroom, children can develop basic skills and concepts. Organized by themes and concept areas, these 50+child and classroom tested recipes will fit naturally into your curriculum.

Easy-to-read, sequential recipe charts will appeal to your children as much as they do to you. Single page formats can easily be copied and sent home for parent follow up.

TABLE OF CONTENTS
- All about Me
- The Seasons
- Colors
- Shapes
- Science
- Opposites
- Math
- Language Development
- Children's Literature
- Celebrations and Holidays

TO ORDER:

Send $9.95 (plus $1 for each book's postage and handling) to:

First Teacher, Inc.
Box 29
60 Main St.
Bridgeport, CT. 06602

OR CALL: 1-800-341-1522

CRAYONS CRAFTS AND CONCEPTS

by
Kathy Faggella

Art activities can teach basic concepts and be integrated into the whole curriculum. Presented in one page, easy-to-read formats, that even your children can follow, these 50+projects will fit into each theme and subject area, you introduce. There are also suggestions for setting up an art area, making smocks, safety rules, and follow ups for each activity. Projects are designed to be reproduced and sent home for follow up, too.

TABLE OF CONTENTS

TO ORDER:

Send $9.95 (plus $1 for each book's postage and handling) to:

**First Teacher, Inc.
Box 29
60 Main St.
Bridgeport, CT. 06602**

OR CALL: 1-800-341-1522

PARTNERS FOR LEARNING

Partners for Learning is based on the belief that parents and teachers are partners in the education of young children. The book is a guide to the development of positive parent participation in schools—from orientation meetings and potluck parent/child meals to parent-sponsored fundraisers and parent volunteer projects. It's a must for the caring classroom!

THINK IT THROUGH

Unique in its organized approach to the teaching of thinking skills to young children, this book offers a great variety of activities for each area of the classroom and curriculum. Each activity develops a specific thinking skill. In addition, there are suggestions for developing creativity and problem-solving skills.

NEW BOOKS from FIRST TEACHER

SPRING '87

SPRING '87

CELEBRATE EVERY DAY

An anthology of the best ideas for celebrations from FIRST TEACHER, this book is based on the experience of hundreds of early childhood teachers. From original ideas for traditional holidays and seasonal celebrations to birthday parties in school and multi-cultural special events, this book will show you how to teach your children that every day is worth celebrating.

BUILDING ON BOOKS

A comprehensive guide to integrating children's literature into all areas of the early childhood curriculum. There are hundreds of annotated book suggestions, each with a motivating or follow-up activity.

TO ORDER:

Send $9.95 (plus $1 for each book's postage and handling) to:

First Teacher, Inc.
Box 29
60 Main St.
Bridgeport, CT 06602

OR CALL:
1-800-341-1522

Q: WHERE CAN YOU FIND HUNDREDS OF CLASSROOM TESTED IDEAS *EACH MONTH* TO HELP YOUR CHILDREN LEARN AND GROW?

A: IN FIRST TEACHER

Each 16 page issue of FIRST TEACHER provides you with innovative projects to make each day an exciting new adventure. We give you ideas for toymaking, games and recipes to do with young children. We take you to the world of make believe with ideas for drama and creative movement. And experts recommend the very best books for young children in FIRST TEACHER.

FIRST TEACHER has a newspaper format, but it's something to read and save. Each issue has a topical theme, so each one adds a permanent resource of projects and ideas to your school or center.

FIRST TEACHER is written by experienced caregivers, daycare directors, and nursery teachers, so it's full of tested ideas to help you guide and motivate young children

FIRST TEACHER has been read and used by over 30,000 Early Childhood teachers. Here's what one of them, Racelle Mednikow, preschool teacher for 16 years, says:

"What a pleasure to be provided with well written, resourceful and usable ideas that can be interjected into our everyday curriculum and be of true value to each of our teachers!"

"Thank you so much for this delightful, informative newspaper."

Subscribe today! Don't miss another month of ideas, projects, and activities.